Baltimore
GHOSTS

HISTORY, MYSTERY, LEGENDS AND LORE

Stories and Photographs by
Ed Okonowicz

Baltimore Ghosts
First Edition

ISBN   1-890690-13-9

Published by
Myst and Lace Publishers, Inc.
1386 Fair Hill Lane
Elkton, Maryland 21921

Printed in the U.S.A.
in Baltimore, Maryland
by Victor Graphics

Typography, Layout and Cover Design
by Kathleen Okonowicz

Dedications

To Cy, Tequila Kid, Logan Street John, Storm Window Harry, Reds,
Jersey Jack, Winney, Chester Tommy, Jessie, Jimmy the Mailman,
Sofia and Freddie, Ed and Bertha, Sambo, J.B., Rosie the Russian,
Your stories are coming.
Ed Okonowicz

To my cousin, Linda Russell
Kathleen Burgoon Okonowicz

Acknowledgments

The author and illustrator appreciate the assistance of those
who have played an important role in this project.

For providing access to the sites
and taking the time to be interviewed:
Vince Vaise, Scott Sheads, John McGarry, Kennedy Hickman,
Jeff Jerome, Lu Ann Marshall, Mary Jo Rodney, Laura Norris, Dee
Williams, Read and Louise Hopkins, Tony Cushing, Indian Timothy,
Beau Reid, Wayne Schaumburg, Robert Mrozek, Larry Pitrof and
Mark Nesbitt.

For sharing their expertise about
haunted sites in the Baltimore area and
providing the HAUR rankings:
Baltimore Society for Paranormal Research officers
Vince Wilson and Robbin Van Pelt.

For their proofreading and suggestions
Barbara Burgoon, Marianna Dyal, Sue Moncure
and Ted Stegura.

Also available from Myst and Lace Publishers, Inc.

Spirits Between the Bays Series

Volume I
Pulling Back the Curtain
(October 1994)

Volume VI
Crying in the Kitchen
(April 1998)

Volume II
Opening the Door
(March 1995)

Volume VII
Up the Back Stairway
(April 1999)

Volume III
Welcome Inn
(September 1995)

Volume VIII
Horror in the Hallway
(September 1999)

Volume IV
In the Vestibule
(August 1996)

Volume IX
Phantom in the Bedchamber
(June 2000)

Volume V
Presence in the Parlor
(April 1997)

DelMarVa Murder Mystery Series

FIRED!
(May 1998)

Halloween House
(May 1999)

Stairway over the Brandywine
A Love Story
(February 1995)

Possessed Possessions
Haunted Antiques, Furniture
and Collectibles
(March 1996)

Possessed Possessions 2
More Haunted Antiques,
Furniture and Collectibles
(September 1998)

Ghosts
(August 2001)

Disappearing Delmarva
Portraits of the Peninsula People
(August 1997)

Friends, Neighbors & Folks Down the Road
(September 2003)

**Terrifying Tales of the
Beaches and Bays**
(March 2001)

**Terrifying Tales 2 of the
Beaches and Bays**
(April 2002)

Table of Contents

Introduction

*There's no more powerful way to stimulate
students to read the works of Edgar Allan Poe
than to tell them a tale as they stand beside the
macabre master's tombstone.*

I t had been too long since I returned to Baltimore. I had
lived in the city for a year during 1970 when I was stationed
at Fort Holabird, a rather small Army base near Dundalk. On
weekends I spent time in the center of town, along Charles
Street, and at neat spots around Highlandtown.

During the following years, my visits were infrequent, usually
rushing past the city along I-95 or taking a day trip to the Inner
Harbor and a museum or concert hall.

Why Baltimore?

When I was ready to write another ghost book, I had to
decide on a focus. Baltimore came to mind. It seemed to offer
everything in the area of legends and stories that a ghost writer
would need—an old wooden sailing ship docked in the Inner
Harbor, the grave and home of horror icon Edgar Allan Poe, and
Fort McHenry, site of the Battle of Baltimore and the writing of
the "Star-Spangled Banner."

Several visits to the Maryland Room at the Enoch Pratt Free
Library yielded stacks of file folders crammed with articles and
columns about haunted locations in Baltimore and throughout
the state of Maryland.

1

I decided a book centered on Baltimore would be well worth the effort. But this time the focus would not be on individual persons' ghost stories and experiences. Instead, the chapters in this book would concentrate on the seaport city's historic sites. And the accompanying ghost tales related to each location would be included in the chapter.

My initial question: "I wonder if there will be enough material?" was answered with the realization that "There's no way I can fit all this stuff into one book!"

I had to make some hard decisions about which places to highlight and which locations to ignore—or at least put aside and save for a follow-up volume.

History Provides the Haunts

The result is a book with an equal distribution of history and haunts. As I mention during every cemetery walk I give and every public talk I present, "The best ghost stories are associated with historical events."

If you want a good spooky story, research the history of a battle, burial site, graveyard, museum or old mansion.

This approach has proved correct during the last eight years as I presented folklore and ghost tales during the evening Ghost/Lantern Tours at Fort Delaware State Park, a fort used as an island prison to hold Confederates during the Civil War.

The history/haunts approach also works well when I offer school and library programs about Delaware and Maryland history.

A distinctive sign welcomes those entering Baltimore along Route 40, from the east.

In this book you will meet curators and historians, saloon-keepers and graveyard guides, ghost hunters and skeptics, all of whom were willing to share spirited tales, unusual incidents and Baltimore's local legends.

What was particularly satisfying is the wealth and variety of types of stories.

The highway ghost along Route 40 is a modified version of a well-known folktale.

A never apprehended phantom that appeared in east Baltimore fills the urban legend category.

Historical haunted stories are featured in the chapters on the *Constellation*, Fort McHenry, Edgar Allan Poe House and Museum and in the saloons in Fells Point.

Cemeteries (and catacombs)—including Green Mount, Westminster and the Fell Plot—served up a full menu of delightful graveyard facts and fantasies.

Of course, Black Aggie, Baltimore's most famous eerie icon, is a creepy chapter that will be read by locals with keen interest. It's also expected that some readers who have had personal experiences related to the statue will be inclined to share their stories. If so, we are eager to receive these tales, and even photographs, for a possible follow-up chapter about readers' individual encounters.

Perhaps the most unusual and satisfying discovery was learning about grave robbing practices operating out of Davidge Hall. This is the original building of the College of Medicine of Maryland, which today is the University of Maryland School of Medicine. Despite the lack of ghost stories associated with this chapter, the story proves that fact is often more horrifying and startling than fiction.

While much of the information in the book has been covered before—whether in newspapers and magazines or in television documentaries—some of the tales have not been spotlighted.

Three such examples include the gallows apparition at Fort McHenry, the ghost face at the bar table at Bertha's in Fells Point, and the dancing spirits that appeared near the brig on a lower deck of the *Constellation*.

To uncover such unusual and little known stories was very satisfying, and I express my appreciation to the cooperative museum curators, business owners and institution employees who gave me their time and were willing to share stories and experiences. Each of them is listed in the particular chapter, and contact information also is provided.

Photographs are another feature in this book. Most were taken during the interviews, and those who work at some of the different locales provided other images.

Myst and Lace Publishers Inc. has produced more than 20 books. Of those, this is the 15th volume dealing with ghosts, legends and history. But it is the first ghost book to use photographs so extensively, a feature that will be included in all upcoming volumes.

Horror and Humor

Without a doubt, below the surface of the modern city of Baltimore there is an old town where mystery is intertwined with its history, like an occult cocktail offering a sip of horror mixed with a hint of dark humor.

Along the cobblestone streets of Fells Point, in the graveyards that surround residential neighborhoods, in the corners and alcoves of historic buildings and beneath the sidewalks beside busy downtown intersections many believe the dead still stir. Some claim that restless phantoms continue to roam or lie in wait, that the spirits of souls that should have moved on have remained behind—and some people say they have witnessed glimpses of beings that have visited them from the other side.

Certain readers will believe what I have written—as it was told to me—and others will not. Whatever conclusions are made are not important. For those who believe in the paranormal, no explanation is necessary. For those who don't believe, no explanation will be satisfactory.

However, what I do hope readers realize is the strong connection between history and mystery, between events and folklore. Also, ghost tales, legends and things that go bump in the night are very useful to teach youngsters about significant events in our country's history.

There's no more powerful way to stimulate students to read the works of Edgar Allan Poe than to tell them a tale as they stand beside the macabre master's tombstone.

Finally, I was unable to include all of the Baltimore stories I had discovered into this one volume, so a follow-up book is a strong possibility. If you have a spooky story or eerie experience that occurred within or near the city that you would like to share, send me a note, an e-mail or call me on the phone. I may include your tale in *MORE Baltimore GHOSTS, History, Mystery, Legends and Lore.*

But, right now I am off to the state capital to uncover legends and ghost stories in and around Annapolis.

If you visit our web site and send us your e-mail, you will be notified of the progress of these and other volumes and my public presentations.

Thanks very much for your interest and for reading our books.

Happy Hauntings

Ed Okonowicz
In Fair Hill, Maryland
at the top of the
Delmarva Peninsula
Fall 2004

New Features in This Book

 Be sure to read the next section about our new **HAUR ranking** that provides a haunted horror rating for each eerie site.

Educators will want to check out page 124 for information about our **Teacher's Guide**, featuring exercises and activities that will help when using this book in the classroom.

Just How Haunted Is It?

'I always tell people, you have to look at the history first.'—Vince Wilson, President, Baltimore Society for Paranormal Research

As we all know, there's haunted and there's HAUNTED!!!! Spooky sites can range from electrical malfunctions and creaking floorboards to apparitions captured on film and electronic voice phenomena (EVP) preserved on a tape or digital recorder. Then, of course, there are those first-person, "I swear I saw it with my own eyes" reports.

In order to offer some perspective on the level of hauntings at the public locations in this book, we have obtained the help of Vince Wilson, cofounder and president of the Baltimore Society for Paranormal Research (BSPR) and the Maryland Paranormal Investigators Coalition (MD-PIC). For several years, his organizations have been investigating reports of unexplained activity at locations in the city and surrounding area.

The society's members have explored unusual phenomena in old saloons, forts, cemeteries, museums, public buildings and private residences.

According to Vince, who lives in Highlandtown area of the city, the connection between history and hauntings is important, and each area of study reinforces the other.

"Baltimore is important," he said,"because so many historical events of significance to our country occurred here. With a number of important historical figures involved, and assuming that hauntings are real—and I believe they are—how could there not be a large amount of spirited activity here?"

BSPR and MD-PIC technical adviser Robbin Van Pelt agreed.

"As technology advances and becomes more economical and readily available to investigators," she said, "the potential is much greater for finding proof of the existence of ghosts."

Photo by Katherine Fowler

MD-PIC officers (from left to right) are Rosemary Ellen Guiley (adviser), Vince Wilson (president), Mary Duvall (treasurer), Robbin Van Pelt (technical adviser), Scott Fowler (secretary) and Jamie Lee Henkin (vice president).

For the first time in our books, each chapter will contain a tombstone chart indicating the site's Haunt and Unexplained Reports rating (HAUR, pronounced "horror").

The HAUR scale reflects BSPR's recommendations based on a variety of factors, such as frequency of reports, on-site investigations, stories and legends, orb count, photographs, EVP, temperature readings, historical events, press and media reports, potential and overall interest in the location.

Rating Levels

The level of unexplained activity will range from a low of 1 tombstone (stating the site is "active") to a top rating of 5 tombstones (for locations with "serious hauntings" or "significant potential"). A place with no haunting history, the site of a legend or one with lack of information—to the society's present knowledge—will bear the "NYR" (not yet rated) designation.

Hopefully, those interested in conducting investigations or visiting these public locations will find the ratings helpful.

For information about the Baltimore Society for Paranormal Research, including training sessions, meeting sites, investigations and events, visit the web site at www.marylandparanormal.com, or send Vince an e-mail message at vwjr.md@verizon.net

Sightings have been reported in this cell, where Private John Drew committed suicide.

Ghostly Gallows at Fort McHenry

'There's a point where the ghost stories and the folk-lore become a part of history.'—Vince Vaise, Park Ranger, Fort McHenry

I was slightly embarrassed when I had to ask for directions to Fort McHenry. For almost my entire life, I have lived only an hour from the historic site, but I had never taken the opportunity to visit its hallowed ground.

Birthplace of our national anthem, site of the defense of Baltimore in the War of 1812 and the only national park in the country that has also been designated an historic shrine are three reasons that a trip to the Patapsco River fort should be on every American's short list of places to see.

Eventually, my hunt for ghost stories led me to the 43-acre, park-like shrine, which has been described as "an oasis" situated on the edge of Baltimore.

On a cold spring afternoon, Park Ranger Vince Vaise, a Baltimore native, treated me to a special tour. As we walked through the sallyport (large, hall-like fort entrance), he offered his perspective on the connection between ghosts (or folklore, as the educators like to say) and history.

"We have a number of ghost tales associated with Fort McHenry," Vince explained. "And while we don't want to be known as a haunted fort, there's a point where the ghost stories and the folklore become a part of history."

9

Over the years—through documentaries, such as The History Channel's *Haunted Baltimore*, and numerous newspaper and magazine articles, including an autumn 1986 issue of the *National Parks* magazine—tales of unusual events at the Baltimore fortification have been reported and discussed.

Having worked with historians at Fort Delaware for nearly 10 years, I was well aware of the strong connection between history and haunts. But from my interviews with present and former staff members at Fort McHenry, there is little doubt that the centuries-old fort has its fair share of things that go bump in the night.

HISTORY

Before we begin the ghost tales, and there are several to share, it's important to understand Fort McHenry's significance and the role it played in our country's early years.

Every school age youngster knows the story of Francis Scott Key—the Baltimore lawyer who witnessed the 25-hour bombardment from the deck of a ship on September 12 and 13, 1814.

It was during the attack—when the British fleet fired between 1,500 and 1,800 shells at the fort—that the mammoth 30- x 42-foot flag made by Mary Pickersgill remained flying high above the fort for all to see.

Key was so inspired by the sight that he took out his pen and began writing the stirring poem that would serve as the words to our national anthem.

Like the British fleet, the Crown's attacking land forces meeting extensive entrenchments on the outskirts of Baltimore, decided to withdraw. Therefore, on September 15, the frustrated attackers retreated and sailed south through the Chesapeake Bay.

While Fort McHenry would never experience another attack, it remained active as a political and military prison during the Civil War. During the latter years of World War I and afterwards, a 3,000-bed Army hospital was located around the fort.

In 1925, Congress designated Fort McHenry as a national park, and in 1939 it was re-designated the nation's only historic site with the double distinction of being both a national monument and historic shrine.

HAUNTS

If it's true that tragedy, death and sudden unfortunate events contribute to the presence of wandering spirits or ghosts, Fort McHenry has good reason to be haunted.

Clagett's Bastion

During the British bombardment, on September 13, 1814, an incoming bomb exploded on the gun emplacement at "Bastion 3." The direct hit killed members of the Maryland militia—an officer named Lieutenant Levi Clagett and John Clemm, a sergeant, both were Baltimore merchants. Some people think it is Clagett's spirit that appears at that site and also walks along the ramparts.

Also referred to as "Clagett's Bastion," the location is one of the five points that juts out from the star-shaped fort. Visitors and employees have reported seeing a soldier, wearing a uniform appropriate to the 1814 era, walking in that area.

A natural reaction to the sighting is to think that the figure in uniform is an actor or re-enactor. However, when informed that there were no performers in costume on the grounds on that particular day, the visitors who reported the sightings usually seem more than a little surprised.

Years ago, park staff that worked in a two-story building inside the fortification, which for years served as an enlisted

Ghosts have been reported in and near Clagett's Bastion, where a British bomb exploded and killed members of the Maryland militia.

men's barracks, have claimed to see a figure dressed in white walking on the building's second floor. They also have reported hearing heavy footsteps, being disturbed by doors and windows being slammed shut and left open, and also finding furniture moved and left out of place.

In *Fort McHenry, Home of the Brave*, author Norman Rukert details an incident involving a park ranger who saw a shadow of a soldier in front of the building that overlooked the spot where Clagett died from the explosion. The ranger took care to verify that it was not his shadow, but also determined that there was no one else in the area that would have cast the phantom specter.

There's also a report that in 1974, while checking out the fort in preparation for a visit by then President Gerald R. Ford, Secret Service agents spotted a uniformed figure on one of the building's porches—but the unexplained sighting occurred after they had sealed the fort and had made sure it was clear of visitors.

Standing at Bastion 3, Vince said that a lot of people think that Fort McHenry only was involved with the War of 1812. He explained that the fort's history begins in the late 1700s, and that it was active until 1923, when it was one of the Army's largest hospitals, with approximately 3,000 beds for returning World War I veterans. Its current general appearance reflects the way the fort looked in the 1870s.

"A lot of military posts have legends," Vince said. "Over the years, the stories become part of each site's history. I think that during the Civil War, the troops probably sat here at Fort McHenry and told ghost stories and legends about the Revolutionary War and War of 1812."

Gallows in the mist

Outside the walls of the fort, in a large open field located near the park entrance, stands the 24-foot-tall statue of Orpheus, the Greek mythological figure associated with poetry and music.

The statue was erected after Congress appropriated funds in 1914 to mark the centennial of the writing of the "Star-Spangled Banner" and the successful defense of Baltimore.

One of the most unusual ghost sightings at Fort McHenry involves an object, the Orpheus statue, and an event, the Civil War, which at first might seem to have little in common.

Scott Sumpter Sheads has been a park ranger at Fort McHenry since 1979. Also a noted historian, he has written several books, among them *Fort McHenry: A History, Fort McHenry and Baltimore's Harbor Defenses* and *Baltimore During the Civil War.*

But while Scott has some interest in folklore and how a story relates to history, he's more concerned with finding the origin of specific folktales and anecdotes. He admitted that he's not involved in sharing ghost stories for the sake of entertainment or amusement, and that he hasn't spent much time following up on reports at the fort that are claimed to be unexplained.

But as we sat in an office, which had once housed enlisted soldiers and their families, he recalled one particular, and rather fascinating, incident that was reported directly to him 18 years ago.

"A lady came up to me in November," Scott said. "It was a foggy day and she was visibly shaken."

He recalled that the woman was in her 50s, well spoken, and that she told him an unusual story that he had never heard before.

She said, "I hope you don't think I'm crazy, but I saw what appeared to be a soldier."

When Scott asked where, the woman pointed toward the area of the Orpheus statue. Then she said, "But the man was not on the ground, he appeared to be in a uniform, but floating above the ground, in the air."

Scott said he thanked the woman and told her he would make a note of it.

The area near the statue of Orpheus has been the scene of a very unusual unexplained incident.

13

However, he did not mention that her sighting had occurred where the gallows had stood during the Civil War. Nor did he explain that her mysterious soldier could be the ghost of Private Joseph Kuhne, who was executed on March 7, 1862.

According to the military records, Kuhne, who was from Co. F, Second Maryland Regiment, U.S.A., had been charged and found guilty for the murder of Second Lieutenant, J. Davis Whitson.

As reported in Scott's book, *Baltimore During the Civil War*, a wooden scaffold was erected outside the Star Fort on the parade grounds and a black walnut coffin was placed beneath it. Nearly 4,000 federal troops arrived, and residents of Baltimore came to witness the "grim display of a military execution—the first ever at Fort McHenry."

In *The Sun* newspaper account reprinted in Scott's book, the ceremony was reported in the rather flowery style of the period:

> "Shortly after twelve o'clock there emerged a wagon from the gateway of the fort guarded by a strong military force. The condemned man was in the wagon, and the procession moved with slow and solemn tread towards the dread instrument of death, the while the accompany band played the 'Dead March'. . . .
>
> "The rope was adjusted on the neck of Kuhne by the acting provost marshal, who read the finding of the court-martial and the death warrant. . . . In another instant the trip fell with a dull, heavy sound, and Joseph Kuhne was suspended in mid-air . . . the drop was only about eighteen inches but for a few moments no motion was observable. After which his contortions were horrible for a minute, after which he hung still and lifeless. . . ."

Perhaps it was Joseph Kuhne's spirit that the park visitor reported seeing that day. There is no way to tell. But this story is a fine example of an historic event serving as the basis for a ghost story or sighting.

While walking the fort earlier in the morning, Vince had mentioned that some people have claimed that "on misty days a gallows appears in the area of the Orpheus statue," which was the site of the original hangman's tower during the Civil War.

Sightings in the barracks

A woman looking out from a second floor window and footsteps on the porch of the enlisted soldiers' quarters have been reported on several occasions, Vince said.

One of the best stories related to the two-story barrack buildings that stand within the walls of the fort came from a Maryland artist. He said he had been doing research at Fort McHenry for an historical painting he was preparing to create.

David (not his real name) said he wanted to make his work as realistic as possible, and he had received permission to review some of the park's historical documents. As he walked through a small doorway that required him to duck, he said, "I got hit like I was struck with a frying pan. It was while I was going through the doorframe. I mean, I was out cold. I was gone, out like a light."

David said he knew at the time that he had not simply bumped his head against the top of the frame or accidentally tapped into a low beam.

The artist said when the park ranger escort returned, he was surprised at the force of the attack, but did not seem shocked that an unusual event had occurred.

"That's our resident ghost," the ranger told David, and then the park worker shared his own story about being pushed down the stairs by a woman dressed in early 19th-century clothing.

David said that it is believed that the ghost had been a sergeant's wife, and that her hus-

A woman has been seen looking out from the second floor windows.

15

band and two children had died from a plague or epidemic that occurred in Baltimore during the 1820s.

Shifting back to his personal attack experience, David said, "I had no cuts, no bruises, no lumps, no nothing. But it was powerful. I hit my knees, and I was face first down on the floor. I attribute it to the lady ghost."

John McGarry, executive director of the Muskegon County Museum in Michigan, worked from 1978-1983 as a park ranger at Fort McHenry.

He recalled noticing activity in the same building, including footsteps around the stairs and in the empty rooms.

"As I recall," he said, "that room [mentioned by the artist] was occupied by a sergeant and his family. When they lost the kids to cholera or typhoid, it's believed the wife went a little wacko. I suspected it was her."

Restless John Drew

Perhaps the fort's most often told haunted tale involves the restless spirit of 28-year-old Private John Drew, who had been assigned to guard duty along the fort's outer battery on November 14, 1880. Unfortunately, the young soldier was discovered in the morning asleep at his post.

Private John Drew was found dead in his cell, located in the section of the building behind the barrel. Many believe his ghost is the most active apparition at the fort.

Embarrassed at failing in his duty and at being arrested, Drew was ordered to a cell in the guard house, which is located in the entrance building containing the sallyport. One can only imagine what went through the young man's mind. His army career was over. His comrades would never give him any respect. He would have a black mark on his military record.

Perhaps these and other considerations caused the young soldier to take drastic and fatal action.

Somehow, Drew was able to smuggle a musket into his cell. Soon after locking the prisoner up, the guards heard a shot from the area of Drew's confinement. When they unlocked the barred metal door, they found that Drew had placed the muzzle of the weapon in his mouth and had used his toe to pull the trigger.

Drew committed suicide, and it's possible his restless soul has never found peace and is serving an appropriate sentence, standing eternal guard duty over Fort McHenry.

Visitors claim they have felt a distinct chill in the cell where Drew took his life. Others say they have sighted a figure— dressed in a long watch coat or cape and wearing a military style cap—walking the same outer battery where the young soldier had been assigned more than 120 years ago.

Author Rukert reported the tale of a park ranger's dog that halted at the exact spot on the seawall where Drew was discovered derelict in his duty. The dog growled and fussed, as if it sensed an unseen presence, then ran off apparently seeking a less troubling site.

John McGarry said that after hearing reports of a phantom guard, they researched what type of uniform John Drew would have been wearing while he was on watch duty. The descriptions of the person in the sightings, he said, seemed to indicate the ghost was wearing the appropriate clothing of that period.

The former park ranger said he spent the 100th anniversary of John Drew's death sleeping in the same jail cell where the private had committed suicide, but nothing significant happened.

John said he remembered that during his time at Fort McHenry a psychic investigator made several trips throughout the fort, searching for indications of unusual activity.

"There were always some kinds of tantalizing clues of psychic phenomena," he said, referring to the psychic's investigations. "If you believe in that stuff, and with the fort as old as it

17

was, and with the battles and incidents related to the war, it's not unusual for some indications to creep in and make their presence known."

John recalled an evening when he was closing the fort for the day and he saw a figure standing in the guardhouse. John called out, "Is that you John Drew?"

The response was a distinct tap on the window, indicating perhaps an answer to the request.

Commenting on his direct and open approach to the possibilities of spirited activity, John said, "These are things that have happened to me, and I can't explain why. I'm comfortable in my faith. A lot of things can't be explained. I would rather take a look at other possibilities than to simply deny their existence."

How the haunts began

Most park staff members seem to agree that the more intense interest in ghosts at Fort McHenry was a direct result of a series of Halloween events that were conducted several decades ago.

While these ghost tours were popular, park administrators, who did not want the historic shrine to be labeled "the haunted fort," discontinued them. Instead, they said the emphasis should be on the hallowed site's significant role in America's history.

The ghost tours are no longer held, but interest in Fort McHenry's phantoms persists. Perhaps this is because of John Drew, Levi Clagett, Joseph Kuhne and other unnamed specters who continue to be sighted and their presence felt at the birthplace of the "Star-Spangled Banner."

For more information about Fort McHenry's schedule, programs and volunteer opportunities, call (410) 962-4290.

Interesting facts

Fort McHenry's distinguished history began in 1776, during the Revolutionary War, as an earthen, star-shaped fortification. It was called Fort Whetstone, named for its location on Whetstone Point. The site was located far enough from Baltimore to provide protection without endangering the city. Since it was surrounded on three sides by water, enemy ships would have to pass the fort before sailing into Baltimore.

A new brick fort constructed in 1803 was named after James McHenry, who was a Maryland representative to the Constitutional Convention and who served on George Washington's staff and was the first president's secretary of war. McHenry attended New Ark Academy, in Newark, Delaware, which later became the University of Delaware.

During the Battle of Baltimore, Francis Scott Key jotted notes on September 14 while on a truce ship. But he did not finish the poem until he returned to Baltimore on September 16. His inspirational work was first entitled "Defence of Fort McHenry." It was published the next day and was sung to the tune of "To Anacreon in Heaven."

Each spring the U.S. Coast Guard places the "Francis Scott Key" buoy in the Patapsco River, near the Key Bridge, marking the location of the ship where the author or the "Star-Spangled Banner" was anchored during the bombardment of Fort McHenry. The special buoy—decorated with red, white and blue stripes, with white stars on a field of blue—is removed in the fall and replaced each spring.

Photo courtesy National Park Service, Fort McHenry NM&HS

The arched entrance of Fort McHenry leads to the area inside the brick walls of the fortification. There visitors will find the flagpole that supports the large American flag, a replica of the symbol that inspired the writing of the "Star-Spangled Banner."

"The Star-Spangled Banner" became the national anthem of the United States in 1931.

Major George Armistead, in charge of the defense of Fort McHenry, wanted its flag to be large enough "that the British will have no difficulty seeing it from a distance." It was 30 feet by 42 feet and made by Mary Pickersgill. It is displayed in the Smithsonian Institution's National Museum of American History in Washington, D.C.

A full size replica of the flag is flown over the fort during days when weather allows.

During the Civil War, Union troops were stationed at Fort McHenry to help keep Baltimore out of the hands of Marylanders who wanted to join the Southern rebellion. The fort's guns were turned toward the city, and the fort was used as a temporary prison where political prisoners, suspected of being Confederate sympathizers were held, often without trial.

Following the Battle of Gettysburg in July 1863, nearly 7,000 Confederate soldiers were held as prisoners in the fort.

In 1917, the United States Army used the fort grounds for U. S. General Hospital No. 2 to care for returning wounded veterans of World War I. It was the largest military hospital in the United States with over 100 temporary buildings. Eventually, the hospital was no longer needed and in 1927 it was torn down.

In 1933 Fort McHenry was made a national park, and in 1939 it was designated a national monument and historic shrine.

During World War II, the fort served as a U.S. Coast Guard Training Center for fire control and port defense.

Two of the error-based but most asked questions offered by visitors at Fort McHenry are: "Is that a statue of Francis Scott Key?" while pointing to the statue of Orpheus and "Is that the Betsy Ross flag that flew over Fort Sumpter during the Civil War?"

Sources:

Rafael Alvarez, "Oh, say, can you see ghosts at fort?" *The Baltimore Sun*, October 31, 1996

P. M. Callaghan, "Fort McHenry has the Spirit," October 1980

James Carman, "GHOST Stories," *National Parks*, September/October 1986

"Coast Guard Cutter James Rankin Marks Historic Site," Homeland Security Press Release, U. S. Coast Guard, May 5, 2004

Fort McHenry National Monument and Historic Shrine brochure, National Park Service

Fort McHenry National Monument and Historic Shrine, http://www.bcpl.net/~etowner/patriot.html

Norman G. Rukert, *Fort McHenry, Home of the Brave*

Scott Sumpter Sheads and Daniel Carroll Toomey, *Baltimore During the Civil War*

Interview, Park Rangers Vince Vaise and Scott Sheads, March 22, 2004

Interview, John McGarry, executive director of the Muskegon County Museum in Michigan, April 2004

Interview, Maryland artist, April 2004

A large American flag flies above the top of Federal Hill.

What's Under the Ground?

'When people think back several years and try to remember their youth and the places they have visited, they sometimes combine the experiences and the facts.'—Vince Vaise, Park Ranger, Fort McHenry

Tourists and residents climb the steps leading to the top of Federal Hill. The elevated location, beneath the large American flag, offers a spectacular view of the Inner Harbor and the city of Baltimore. But there is a fascinating legend associated with the popular site, and it's a story that both visitors and locals might find surprising. But first let's learn a little about the hill's history.

History

It's believed the first explorer to sight the tall mound was Captain John Smith, who had sailed from Jamestown, Virginia, to explore areas to the north. In June 1606, he ended a short journey at the Patapsco River where he saw "a great red bank of clay flanking a natural harbor basin." Originally, Baltimore settlers called this large mound "John Smith's Hill."

During its history, the well-known landmark has hosted major celebrations, aided maritime commerce and navigation, and served the state and country in time of war.

In May 1788, thousands of Baltimoreans celebrated Maryland's ratification of the U.S. Constitution at the site, and they moored a 15-foot replica of a sailing ship, named the

Federalist, at the base of the hill. Soon thereafter, the name Federal Hill caught on and it remains to this day.

In 1795, taking advantage of the hill's high vantage point and extensive sight line, a maritime observatory and signal tower were erected at the top, allowing a dozen-mile panorama down the Patapsco River.

During the War of 1812, a signal gun was established at Federal Hill to alert the city and harbor about potential British attack. But since the British advances failed at both Fort McHenry and at Hampstead Hill (now a city park called "Patterson Park"), the Federal Hill artillery guns were not fired. The signal gun on Federal Hill, however, did alert the city and Fort McHenry to the initial British land advance at the eastern part of the city.

In April 1861, immediately after the Baltimore Riots—when the city's Southern sympathizers attacked Union troops near the President Street Railroad Station—federal troops occupied the hill and established barricades and artillery at what became known as Federal Hill Fort.

The site was turned into a public city park in 1880, and in the 1970s the surrounding neighborhood, identified as "Federal Hill District," was named to the National Register of Historic Places. Today the Federal Hill area remains a popular locale, accented by restored homes, plus popular restaurants, taverns and shops that are patronized by tourists and residents.

Legends

Some element of truth is usually the basis for any good story, even those dealing with the unexplained. In the case of Federal Hill, the truth lies, literally, beneath the surface of the story and below the "great red bank of clay" itself.

While talking to Vince Vaise and Scott Sheads, park rangers at Fort McHenry, they both mentioned the "urban legends associated with the tunnels under Federal Hill."

During the 19th century, miners dug short tunnels beneath the hill to extract fine white sand used to make glass. Workers also hauled away red clay and used it for sash weights for windows, and some can still be found in the nearby neighborhood structures.

During the Civil War, Scott said, the Union troops stored gunpowder in the tunnels beneath Federal Hill Fort.

24

Old tunnels, and even some entrances to the abandoned mines located under Federal Hill, have been discovered in cellars of area homes and businesses.

The top of Federal Hill offers a marvelous view of the Inner Harbor and the city of Baltimore.

The urban legend, however, Vince added, is that the Civil War tunnels beginning at Federal Hill connected with Fort McHenry. There are even stories that the tunnels extended all the way to Fort Carroll (in the middle of the Patapsco River) and to the Washington Monument (across the Inner Harbor, in the center of the city).

"They said the Union troops used the subterranean passages to secretly go from one place to another," Vince said. "But, since the Union troops controlled the city, they didn't have to use tunnels." If anything, he added, it would have been the Confederates who needed to travel secretly and make use of the mysterious underground network.

Vince said the legends of the tunnels gained some credibility in the 1950s, when a nearby row house caved into one of the old mining tunnels.

Despite denials and explanations that it would be physically impossible for the tunnels to be long enough to reach all of the mentioned sites—and that they would have to be dug under the shipping channels—some people still believe they exist on a grand scale.

Vince said he has heard such explanations as, "My grandfather told me that he walked through them." Sometimes when Vince has tried to explain the actual situation, people have gotten upset and replied, "That's what the government wants you to say."

"But that's natural," Vince said. "When people think back several years and try to remember their youth and the places they have visited, they sometimes combine the experiences and the facts."

According to the web site Federal Hill Online, because the temperature in the tunnels is cool, nearby breweries stored kegs of beer at the site.

But rumors persist of children having been lost in the underground labyrinths and of the hidden passageways that were used during Prohibition to hide and transport illegal booze.

Even today, some claim that in the basements of homes and in the cellars of old businesses, behind boarded up entranceways there are secret mazes that you can follow that eventually will end up at . . . Fort McHenry, the Washington Monument and who knows where else within, and beyond, the city.

Sources

William Doane Jr., "Federal Hill," *The Baltimore Sun*, November 10, 1999

Federal Hill Online, http://www.federalhillonline.com/history/htm

Federal Hill Underground Tunnels, Maryland Ghost & Spirit Association, http://www.marylandghosts.com/phpbb/viewtopic.php?t=163

Interview, Park Ranger Vince Vaise and Park Ranger Scott Sheads, March 22, 2004

USS Constellation is a must-see tourist attraction located in Baltimore's Inner Harbor.

Seafaring Spirits in the Inner Harbor

'Whatever may be the explanation of these phenomena the sentences which Simmons has received will tend to discourage the men from giving undue publicity to their supernatural observations.'—Yeoman Moses Safford, USS *Constellation*, June 20, 1863

I n the shadows of glitzy metal towers and beside the hurried flow of passing traffic it sits, a solitary wooden relic of times long passed. To some, it offers a hint of history; to others it suggests more than a trace of mystery.

Because of its age and tall masts and rigging, its sturdy cannons and polished decks, there's a possibility that some of its unsettled tales have been the result of fertile imaginations.

But still, more than a few staff members are unable to explain some rather unusual experiences that just might have been caused by . . . ghosts.

Welcome aboard USS *Constellation*, a Baltimore treasure.

Early History

It's important for readers and ship visitors to understand that there were two wooden-hulled vessels christened USS *Constellation*. The first was a frigate built in Baltimore and launched in 1797. It served the country battling French ships and privateers. After the War of 1812, it patrolled along the Atlantic Coast and sailed into the Mediterranean Sea to fight the Barbary Coast pirates. In the 1820s and 1830s, the frigate's mission was to fight piracy and interdict slave ships trying to enter the U.S. with their human cargo.

29

This original ship, the U.S. Frigate *Constellation*, was in active service until 1845, and it was broken up in 1853. Among her commanders was Captain Thomas Truxtun, who directed *Constellation's* battle against the French ships *L'Insurgente* and *La Vengeance*.

The second *Constellation*, the ship currently on display in Baltimore's Inner Harbor, is a sloop-of-war that was launched in 1855, only a few years before the outbreak of the Civil War.

Between 1859-1861, USS *Constellation* served as flagship of the U.S. African Squadron, patrolling off the mouth of the Congo River for ships participating in the illegal slave trade. During this cruise, *Constellation* captured three slave ships, freeing 705 captives. With the outbreak of the Civil War, *Constellation* was ordered to the Mediterranean, where it protected American commerce from Confederate raiders and showed the flag to keep up foreign relations.

Following the War Between the States, USS *Constellation* served in a number of roles, one as a training ship for midshipmen at the U.S. Naval Academy at Annapolis, Maryland. In 1880, it was used to deliver supplies to Ireland as part of the efforts of the Irish Relief Fund.

During the subsequent decades, the ship was used primarily for training and ceremonial purposes. But since the mid 1950s, it has had a visible presence in the city of Baltimore.

Haunts

Ask any city resident to name Baltimore's most haunted sites and, without hesitation, many will begin to share stories about the USS *Constellation*.

Since the ship was first made accessible to Inner Harbor tourists, there have been rumors, urban legends and speculation about ghosts roaming over, under, around and through the vessel's decks. Certainly, much of this fascination is because ghost stories and legends seem to be automatically attached to old ships, and USS *Constellation* is about as old as you can get.

Reports of paranormal sightings on the upper and lower decks of the floating Baltimore museum have been printed in newspapers and magazines and also featured in The History Channel documentary *Haunted Baltimore*. But, while speaking to Kennedy Hickman, curator/historian for the USS *Constellation*

Museum, he said if there are any ghosts aboard, these spirits seem to be roaming a ship other than the one on which they had served.

According to Ken, the current ship is believed to have very little material used in its construction from the original Baltimore built frigate. Nevertheless, several stories seem to have taken on a life of their own, and they all are associated with the first vessel. They include the tales of Neil Harvey, Captain Truxtun and a young boy that died on a lower deck.

Neil Harvey was a member of the frigate crew. During an engagement in 1799, while the ship was in the West Indies and during the year of its battle against the French ship *La Vengeance*, Harvey supposedly ran from his post in battle.

This was a serious offense, and there are several endings to Harvey's maritime career. The sailor was hung, or he was run through with a sword or he was blown up. The last option, Ken explained, was more gruesome. Essentially, the unlucky man was strapped to the front of a cannon and then blasted apart.

In the 20th century, the ghostly figure of Neil Harvey—with his limbs all found and replaced in the correct locations—has been reported floating across the decks of the ship.

A cannon located on the Constellation's deck

Commander Thomas Truxtun is said to be the ship's second resident ghost. The U.S. Congress presented the frigate's late 18th-century captain a medal for his excellent command of *Constellation* during battles against the French in 1799 and 1800. But, in modern times, the old salt has been credited with giving special tours of the ship.

In 1964, one day, late in the afternoon, a Catholic priest was leaving the ship and passed a few staff members who were closing up the museum. The reverend paused to compliment the staff on the fine presentation he had just received from a costumed guide on one of the lower decks.

The staff members, who knew they had no interpreter working on the vessel at that time, went aboard and inspected the

31

entire ship. They found no one else—in or out of a late 18th-century naval uniform—on board.

Truxtun was not from Baltimore, and he died elsewhere. So one would tend to wonder why the commander of the original frigate *Constellation* would want to spend a fair part of his eternity in Baltimore harbor, offering free, guided sightseeing trips on a vessel upon which he had never served.

Boys and young men served on sailing ships as messengers, cook's helpers, officer's aides, ammunition carriers and sick bay attendants. (During the Civil War, young men between the ages of 13 and 18 could join the Navy and work as Boys or Apprentices. Often, due to their small size, they carried cartridges to the guns and were able to scurry below decks rather easily. They were called "powder monkeys.")

It's said one small boy, who served on the ship in the 1820s, was killed below decks. There is no reason given. It could have been an accident, a game or prank gone awry or even a murder or beating. Nevertheless, there have been reports of a young phantom appearing to visitors at various times.

The top deck of the ship where a ghostly sailor is reported to roam

In 1955, the *Baltimore Sun* published a blurred photograph of a naval officer marching across the deck of the ship.

The photo is reported to have been taken by a U.S. Navy officer who had set up his camera on a tripod on the top deck. The story states, "At 11:59 P.M., to be exact, the Navy officer 'detected a faint scent in the air—a certain something not unlike gunpowder.'

"Then before him, he said, appeared a 'phosphorescently glowing, translucent ectoplasmic manifestation of a late Eighteenth Century sailor, complete with gold striped trouser, cocked hat and sword.' He barely had time to snap the shutter before the eerie figure vanished, he said."

After this attention-grabbing picture appeared in the daily newspaper, the common-held belief that the ship was haunted was reinforced a hundred-fold.

Another story involved workmen doing repairs on the ship. They said they heard strange sounds coming from the lower decks. But each time they went below to investigate the source of the noise, they found no one on the ship.

When asked about the presence of ghosts on *Constellation*—and it is a question that is posed quite often—Ken said, "We try to politely debunk the stories." He added that people who have worked at the museum know that these old ghost stories were manufactured in the 1960s and 1970s to attract attention to the ship.

However, he added, there is one tale that is significantly different from the legends. This story has a tangible historical link, and it is one that even the curator and other staff members find fascinating and maybe even believable.

It's in the diary

The account involves an entry in a copy of the *Diary of Yeoman Moses Safford, USS Constellation, 1862-1865.*

The statement about a paranormal incident is dated June 20, 1863, when Moses Safford, a lawyer from Kittery, Maine, was the ranking staff petty officer. He was in charge of equipment and supplies for the maintenance and operation of the ship. Stafford wrote:

A copy of Safford's Diary

"Ike Simmons, the negro cook's mate was given five days in the brig in double irons for singing last night in the same place where he was being confined for another offense. According to 'Ike,' Nichols, the negro, and Raynes, the Kanaka, who died recently on the ship, appeared before him and danced in the brig outside of his cell and he sang to them. The ship's corporal told me as something which was puzzling him that this morning he found in the brig five buckets stacked up in a peculiar way and which had stood up in spite of the motion of the ship. Simmons was in the cell and could not have stacked them and the corporal had the only key to the door of the brig, which was locked. I am informed the mysterious occurrences or manifestations have annoyed and tested the nerves of men who have been confined in the brig before. Some of these incidents have been mentioned only to the Master-at-arms. Twice on stormy nights last fall, Campbell, the captain of the forecastle, whom we lost in the Atlantic, was supposed to have been seen standing near the lee cathead. Whatever may be the explanation of these phenomena the sentences which Simmons has received will tend to discourage the men from giving undue publicity to their supernatural observations." (Safford, D-107)

(John Campbell was listed as lost at sea in 1862.)

The brig was located on this section of flooring shown at the bottom of the photograph.

The written statement that the prisoner (Ike) saw two dead men and that he (Ike) was entertaining them (Nichols and Raynes) with his singing is interesting.

However, the stacked buckets and the appearance of another dead sailor (Campbell) add to the mystery. Finally, the decision to give Ike extra time in the brig for sharing his ghost story—in an effort to "discourage" sharing similar tales by other members of the crew— demonstrates that even a century and a half ago there were attempts to stifle these types of unsettling stories, which could be quite distracting to superstitious members of a crew out at sea.

In his three years working at *Constellation,* Ken said he has not seen, heard or experienced any unexplained events aboard ship. However, a few of the staff members that work in the offices and gift shop area have reported unusual occurrences.

More than once, the figure of a man has been seen in the gift shop, after hours, wandering among the aisles. And then he suddenly disappears.

Books have fallen off the shelves without any logical cause. And one woman said she saw a hazy or foggy figure moving in the corner of her eye.

Why would ghost sailors who had served on the original frigate, that was scrapped and destroyed, decide to haunt a different vessel with the same name?

Perhaps they are in search of a maritime home that is similar to the one on which they spent so much time. Maybe they don't realize their earthly existence is over.

Whoever offers an explanation is providing nothing more than a guess.

But, based on the account in *Safford's Diary,* the sloop-of-war *Constellation's* more believable haunters are the dancing spirits of John Nichols and Charles Raynes, who demanded a spirited tune. And there's also the ghost of John Campbell, who was lost in the Atlantic and whose soul will not rest as long as his body remains in the clutches of the deep.

For more information about the USS Constellation Museum, located at Pier 1, 301 East Pratt Street, call (410) 539-1797 or visit the web site at www.constellation.org

Interesting facts:

The first U.S. Navy ship to bear the name *Constellation,* referring to the "new constellation of stars" on the American flag, was launched in Baltimore on September 7, 1797. Due to its swift speed, it earned the nickname, "Yankee Racehorse."

In the first test against a foreign foe in the undeclared "Quasi War" with France, *Constellation,* with Captain Thomas Truxtun commanding, won the first ship vs. ship victory of the U.S. Navy.

After several overhauls, in 1853, it was deemed that further renovation was not economically effective, and the frigate

Constellation was decommissioned and broken up at the Navy Yard in Portsmouth, Virginia.

With plans completed in May and the keel laid on June 25, 1853, just before steam propulsion was adopted as auxiliary power for all new warships, the second *Constellation* was the last all-sail ship designed by the Navy, as well as the largest "sloop" built to that date.

In 1914, *Constellation* participated in the 100th anniversary celebration of the Battle of Baltimore and Francis Scott Key's poem, which became the national anthem.

In 1917, a new battle cruiser was under construction and christened *Constellation*, to honor its famous predecessor. The historic ship's official name was changed to *Old Constellation* during World War I to prevent confusion in having two ships with the same name. The sloop-of-war reverted to her original name in 1925, when the cruiser was scrapped.

Constellation made a public appearance in Philadelphia, to help commemorate the 150th anniversary of the Declaration of Independence on July 4, 1926.

In 1933, the ship was decommissioned for preservation as a navy relic. However, *Constellation* was recommissioned in 1940,

USS Constellation, circa 1856 (Print provided by the USS Constellation Museum, Baltimore, Maryland, and used with its permission.)

and in 1941 the ship was designated "relief flagship" of Commander-in-Chief of the U.S. Atlantic Fleet.

Following World War II, *Constellation* was towed to the Boston Navy Yard to be placed in "ordinary" (the equivalent of a steel ship being placed in "mothballs"). In 1954, *Constellation*— thought by many to be the original 1797 frigate—was moved to Baltimore for restoration and preservation as an historic shrine by a private, non-profit patriotic organization.

For several decades until the mid 1990s, *Constellation* was open as a museum in the Inner Harbor. However, in 1996 she was involved in a nearly three year, $10 million restoration project.

On July 2, 1999, the reconditioned *Constellation* arrived at her present site in Baltimore's Inner Harbor.

It is the last all-sail powered warship built by the U.S. Navy and the only surviving craft still afloat that actively served her country during the Civil War.

Sources:

Don and Marian Conboy, "Baltimore's Spookiest Ghost Stories," *Baltimore Magazine*, October 1979

Diary of Yeoman Moses Safford, USS Constellation, 1862-1865. Moses Safford

Haunted Baltimore, The History Channel Documentary

"Marylanders compile rich legacy of ghostly tales and legendary lore," *The Sun*, October 31, 1972.

USS CONSTELLATION: A Short History of the Last All-Sail Warship Built by the U.S. Navy, Glenn F. Williams

USS Constellation web site, www.constellation.org

Interview, Kennedy Hickman, curator and historian, USS Constellation Museum, Baltimore, March 22, 2004

The Edgar Allan Poe House, 203 North Amity Street, which the author called "The little house in the lowly street with the lovely name."

Working in the Poe House

'This place gives me the creeps!'—Vincent Price

To some people, Jeff Jerome's job and workplace would be a dream fulfilled. The Baltimore historian spends his days in the small house on Amity Street where Edgar Allan Poe lived, slept, ate, imagined and wrote.

When Jeff ventures up to Poe's third-floor, garret bedroom, he must move over the wooden planks on the narrow, winding stairway. And each time he makes the climb, the Baltimore native is, literally, walking in the footsteps of America's first master of mystery.

Compare that to a workweek spent in a sterile office building with modular furniture, metal cabinets, rows of identical cubicles, ringing phones and crowded elevators.

But that is only the beginning of our adventure into life (and, perhaps, even some evidence of afterlife) at the Poe House and Museum. To gather the complete story, I spent an afternoon with Jeff in the front parlor of, what Poe himself described as, "The little house in the lowly street with the lovely name."

During my interview, I discovered some new details about Edgar Allan Poe, but there was even more fascinating information about the people that have visited Jeff during his 25 years working and greeting guests in the historic building.

Jeff's arrival at the popular tourist site in 1979 was the result of having the right background and being in the right place at the right time.

"It wasn't like as a kid I wanted to be curator of the Poe House," he said, offering me this first of many clever remarks and delightful quips that would accent our three-hour conversation.

With a background in photography, computers and sales, he said he had spent much of his free time studying his true love, local history. During the time of America's Bicentennial, Jeff served as a volunteer conducting tours at Westminster Cemetery, site of Edgar Allen Poe's resting place.

He described the old graveyard as "packed with Baltimore history," featuring Revolutionary War heroes, plus mayors, and a number of famous military leaders. Each, he said, had an important story that he enjoyed sharing.

Eventually, as a result of his knowledge of both area history and of Poe's experiences in the city, Jeff became a resident expert on the famous writer, who lived in Baltimore—briefly in 1829, in Little Italy, and then again from 1832-1835.

When the city decided to restore the Poe House in 1979, officials needed a full time curator and Jeff applied. His expertise on the writer, his experience dealing with tourists at the cemetery and his availability when the opening occurred all worked to his advantage. Jeff became the first and, to date, only curator of the Poe House and Museum historic site.

"I enjoyed meeting people," he said, thinking back to his early days at the house. "I enjoyed talking about Baltimore history and learning about Poe. I used to think, if this kind of work would only pay, I could do this."

House and the history

Jeff said he has had conversations with experts who have an enormous knowledge about Poe—including hopeful young writers and some of the country's most famous celebrities, such as Vincent Price and Stephen King. But he also has talked to visitors with very little knowledge of the writer, and they often have a number of misconceptions about Poe.

"They think Poe was a drunk or a drug addict," Jeff said, "or that he robbed graves to get his story ideas. That's the

Hollywood image. My work here is to talk about the truth related to Poe. Even in the beginning, I saw a need to tell people the other side of Poe's life, his real story."

And throughout the year they come, to see the small house, to discover what is inside, to take pictures, to ask Jeff questions (of all types) and to be able to return home and tell their friends they were "inside the Poe House."

Busses pull up, dropping off school groups and seniors. Charter coaches traverse the narrow street with loads of out-of-town tourists, and taxis deposit foreign visitors from all over the world.

"They range from the ordinary tourist, to some who come here as a pilgrimage," Jeff said.

Surprisingly, perhaps, is the lack of scholars and researchers that make the trip. However, Jeff explained, such serious academics are more interested in researching documents, which the Baltimore home does not contain. So libraries tend to offer more useful material about Poe for those involved in literary studies.

Located about 10 blocks from the Poe gravesite, it's important that visitors understand that during Poe's time at this home it stood in the country. Baltimore's Inner Harbor area was not the

Poe House Curator Jeff Jerome, standing in the former kitchen beside a display featuring portraits of the famous writer and his wife, Virginia

41

center of town in the early 1800s. Instead, Fells Point, located farther to the east, was where all the action occurred.

So Poe would leave his front door in a sparsely populated area that had more fields than homes, more farm animals than folks, and head into Baltimore to sell his words and phrases.

Today, with the expansion of the city and block after block of row homes, it's hard for visitors to imagine how different Baltimore was about 170 years ago.

Reactions to the house can be interesting.

"To a lot of people," he said, "it's not what they imagined they would see. They will tell me, 'It's not what I expected. I thought it would be bigger.' Some expected a much larger house. But then they learn that Poe was poor at this time in Baltimore."

Jeff said he takes the opportunity to explain that "five people starved in a house like this," stressing the meager existence of Poe, his grandmother, his aunt, and his two cousins.

"While some are disappointed," Jeff said, "others have said 'This is exactly like I thought it would be.' Some expect to see manuscripts or Poe letters, or some say they wish there was more furniture. We could have the bones of Poe upstairs on display and they would want more."

Certain visitors, mainly those obsessed with Poe, have become angry during their visits, Jeff said. "They expect to see a shrine, with votive candles and areas roped off. They are upset that we let tourists in and that they are allowed to go through the house. They're upset that we have a video and exhibits. They have come up to me and said, 'You should be fired for desecrating the reputation of Poe.' I sometimes wonder if curators at other museums have experienced similar reactions."

Psychic visitors

It was in the 1980s and early '90s, Jeff said, when there was a flurry of activity and interest from ghost hunters and psychics.

"We haven't had that many calls in the last 10 years," he said, "but in the '80s, every time you picked up the phone, someone wanted information related to hauntings. I used to accommodate them, invited them to come over and do whatever they do, and even opened the house up for them at night. But I was finding out more and more that some of the people weren't sincere in what they were doing."

Jeff said they would come in and immediately report that they "see spirits or they see Edgar walking around," or "I see a man with a mustache coming toward me."

Smiling, Jeff waved his hand and added, "When Poe lived here in 1832 he didn't have a mustache."

Other statements that Jeff has heard confirm that many of the self-proclaimed psychics and ghost hunters mix a heavy dose of imagination into their reporting.

"There are a number of other ways I can tell if they are sincere," Jeff said. "Our policy now is they can come and look for ghosts during the time we are open. But there are no opportunities to be in the building after hours."

Requests for séances and late night investigations have fallen off dramatically, Jeff said, noting that now he only receives about three calls a year.

After acknowledging that his job is unusual, I wondered about the reactions Jeff received when people discovered where he worked and what he did.

The Poe House curator didn't have to think long before responding. One of the best reactions, he said, is when people have told him, "That's so nice of you to donate yourself to help mankind."

Confused at first, Jeff found out that these people thought he had said he worked at the "poor" house. So he is conscious to stress the pronunciation of the word "Poe."

Other responses have included: "What a neat job," and "You're the guy we read about in the newspaper" or "How can you work in such a morbid place?"

Laughing, Jeff added,

The desk and other furniture displayed in Poe's bedroom are reproductions and were not owned by the author.

43

"They think we have a morgue or something in here. But," he continued, "they have this major misconception about Poe. "

Jeff added that when someone discovered he gave tours at the Westminster Cemetery the reactions were similar.

"At first they look at you like you have the plague," he said. "That's their first reaction. Then, when you explain the lives of the heroes buried there, there's a great fascination with what you do and with the place itself."

Memorable moment

A never-to-be-forgotten Poe House incident happened several years ago when three women from Texas called and arranged a private tour of the home, to be held after normal visiting hours.

When the trio arrived, Jeff said, "I opened the door and there were three of the most attractive women I had ever seen. It was obvious they had class, were well mannered, educated and poised. Drop dead gorgeous. At that moment I thought to myself, 'Jeff this is a great job. You made the right decision.' "

Surprisingly, Jeff said, during the tour they all seemed distracted, as if they weren't interested in viewing the rooms or learning about what had occurred during Poe's time in the house.

"You could tell they weren't involved," he said. "You could sense there was something more they wanted."

When one of the women asked if they could see the basement, Jeff led them down. But when they saw the cement floor they were disappointed.

As they were leaving the house, one of the women asked if Jeff would give them a tour of Poe's gravesite, which he realized seemed to have some special interest for them.

Throughout the time in Westminster Cemetery, Jeff said the women were distant whenever he spoke of the other famous people buried there. They only gave him their full attention when he focused on Poe.

"Toward the end of the tour," Jeff remembered, "one of them said, 'Jeff, we have a question for you. But we don't want to offend you.' "

Since he was anticipating an offer to go out for a drink or escort the ladies to a restaurant, Jeff was surprised when she said, "Can we gather up some cemetery dirt?"

"I immediately shouted, 'You're witches!' " Jeff said, laughing as he remembered the event. "I said it before I could think. It just came right out. And they said, 'You're right. But don't worry, we're not going to put a spell on you because you gave us a great tour.' "

The Texas trio assured Jeff that they were white witches and only cast good spells. At that time, the area around Poe's grave was not paved over like it is today. Jeff said that he couldn't stop them from what they desired. They scooped up dirt from around the tomb and placed it in a cloth bag.

Smiling, Jeff recalled they were very satisfied with their visit. "They said, 'Thanks for letting us do this,' and they gave me a big tip."

Meeting the master

In the late 1970s, before the house was renovated, Jeff noticed that actor Vincent Price, who had starred in a number of movies based on Poe's books and stories, was performing in Baltimore. Jeff thought it would be appropriate to invite the noted performer to the Poe House for a private tour. But Jeff had no idea that he would have an opportunity to meet privately with Vincent Price and escort him around Baltimore.

Price's manager arranged a backstage meeting at the Morris Mechanic Theatre. Jeff remembered shaking the actor's hand and being invited to sit and have a private talk.

"He was the nicest guy," Jeff said. "He told me to sit down, and after five minutes we were just like buddies. We clicked. We were talking and relaxed. He was that way with everyone. I invited him to the Poe House."

When Price arrived, reporters representing all the city's television stations and newspapers, who were there to record the event, accompanied him.

Referring to the limited space in the house, Jeff recalled, "This place was jammed, since there's not a lot of room."

A bit later, Price asked Jeff for permission to go into Poe's room—alone.

"We were in there together," Jeff recalled, "and he said, 'Jeff, this place gives me the creeps.'

"I said to him, 'You big baby. You've been in all the horror films.' Then he said, 'I'm honored to be here, to be where Poe wrote his first horror story, where Poe slept. But, Jeff, it gives me the creeps. Let's go.' "

Their next stop was the Westminster Cemetery. Jeff walked beside Price through the catacombs, which is an eerie area under the church that is accented with old vaults, tombstones and mausoleums.

It was during a hushed moment in the catacombs when Price grabbed Jeff's arm. At first the curator thought the actor was unsure of his footing, but he pulled Jeff aside and said, "Jeff, I thought that Poe's house was creepy, but his place takes the cake. Let's get out of here and see Poe's grave."

Jeff said one of his greatest moments of his life was seeing Vincent Price standing at the grave of Edgar Allan Poe. To have played a part in bringing the two legends together is extremely satisfying.

"I feel honored," Jeff said. "Vincent Price was an accomplished actor before he did the Poe films. And those Poe films were responsible for introducing both Poe and Price to a whole new generation of people. And Vincent Price realized the value of that day, of that moment."

Séance on Halloween night

The Poe House reopened after renovations in August 1979. As the result of a suggestion by a friend who worked at a radio station, a séance was held from 11 p.m. to midnight on Halloween night.

With remote equipment set up in the building and outside, five people sat around a wooden table on the second floor. Two policemen and two technicians stood in the background, and another officer was posted outside for security.

The program took place in the larger bedroom, which has the stairway leading to Poe's bedroom. Since it was being broadcast live, Jeff was told by the station producers to keep talking throughout the event. But when Jeff tried to explain that séances are not conducted with non-stop chatter, the radio staff said that didn't matter. On the radio, they stressed, no sound—called dead air—was deadlier than a Poe-inspired death scene. So Jeff said he tried to offer a running commentary for the station's listeners.

After 15 minutes of describing the setting, Jeff was startled when the fellow next to him began squeezing the curator's hand.

"I thought, 'Oh, great. This guy likes me.' "

But Jeff was relieved when he realized that the fellow beside him seemed to have drifted into a trance, and the man started mumbling something about "getting wood" and calling out "Where's Virginia?"

This went on for sometime, all the while Jeff noticed he was receiving disapproving glances from his psychic friend sitting directly across the table. Being new to this type of work, Jeff said he didn't know the protocol or what to expect.

However, at 11:45 p.m., several people—including a few of those at the table, the police officers and the technicians in the room—all looked up suddenly at the stairway, but no one said anything.

Shortly after midnight, as everyone was leaving, Jeff spoke to the psychic and her husband, both of whom had been sitting opposite him. While they casually dismissed the mumbled rantings of the man seated beside Jeff as an obvious lark, they told the curator they were disappointed he would have hidden someone upstairs in Poe's room to make heavy footsteps.

Jeff had no idea what they were talking about. But

The stairs leading to Poe's third-floor bedroom

within moments he learned that at 11:45 p.m. the police, technicians and psychic all had heard the same sounds—someone apparently walking in the room and stomping on the stairs.

"They told me," Jeff recalled, " 'You can tell your friend upstairs to come down now.' But when I assured them there was no one in Poe's room they looked surprised. The next day the psychic called and said she was fully convinced that we made contact with something the previous night. She said she can't be certain it was Poe, but it was something."

Window in the bedroom

There is one strange experience that Jeff has told numerous times, and it is one that was recreated during filming for The History Channel's documentary, entitled *Haunted Baltimore*. The incident involves an actress and a window.

In the mid 1980s, Jeff was working with a performer to do a theatrical presentation of Poe's work, "Bernice." It was to take place inside the historic house. While the part called for a male, the woman was very eager to present the work. She was quite talented and said she was willing to be made up to look like a male for the part.

Just prior to a rehearsal—while she was in the smaller, back bedroom, on the second floor changing into her costume—Jeff was downstairs and heard a crash and a scream.

When he rushed onto the second floor, the woman was standing with her costume pulled against her chest, staring at a large window that was resting in the center of the floor.

"She was terrified," Jeff recalled. "She said, 'I was changing into my costume, thinking about the play. I noticed the window, tilting out. But it kept coming out, stopped for a second, and flew out of the frame and landed right in the center of the room.'

"Then," Jeff added, "standing there half undressed, she said, 'I can't stay here. I cannot do this play,' and she left."

Afterwards, Jeff said he replaced the window and then tried to pull it out of its slot. But it was impossible to remove easily out of the groove.

"There was no way it should have been able to fly across the room," he said. recalling the incident.

This window flew across the room and frightened an actress, who fled from the building.

The next day Jeff called his psychic friend, the one who had been at the séance. After describing what had occurred, the woman told him, "The only thing I can tell you without being there is some entity didn't want her there. That was its way of saying, 'Get out!' "

"To this day," Jeff said, "I'll never be able to explain how that happened."

Jeff said he is asked often for his opinion about spirits at the Poe House.

While there have been a few instances of unusual sounds and seemingly unexplained events, his approach has always been to try to find a logical explanation for anything that cannot be understood initially.

But, he admitted, in a few instances—such as the footsteps during the séance and the window traveling across the room— he still hasn't come up with rational answers.

Sometimes, people wonder if working at the Poe House gives Jeff the creeps, referring to Vincent Price's famous comment.

Smiling, the curator said, "I tell them, I'm in awe. I've got a job in the house where Edgar Allan Poe lived. I'm walking on the floor in the house where he wrote his first horror story. I've met people from around the world, from Vincent Price and Stephen King to students. I'm the luckiest guy in the world."

For more information about the Edgar Allan Poe House and Museum, call (410) 396-7932. Hours are seasonal and it is best to call before making a visit.

Interesting facts

Edgar Allan Poe was a writer of poems and short stories. He also was a literary critic, editor, publisher and lecturer. In fact, in the 1840s, he presented a lecture in Old College, at the University of Delaware in Newark, Delaware. According to a local legend, Poe was thrown out of the Saint Patrick's Tavern on Main Street, and he placed a curse on the building. Two years after Poe's death, the tavern burned down, and locals blame the incident on the Poe Curse. The present establishment, now called the Deer Park, uses a raven as one of its symbols and is proud of its association with Poe.

writer lived from 1832-1835 in Baltimore at what is
known as the Poe House, located at 203 North Amity
Street.

The home was built about 1830, and was saved from demolition in 1941 by the Edgar Allan Poe Society of Baltimore.

The 2-1/2-story brick duplex contains five rooms. The front parlor is the entrance to the home. The former kitchen is used as an exhibition area of assorted items, including a color portrait of Poe's wife, Virginia.

Illustrations of "The Raven" by Gustave Dore are displayed on the second floor, in the room where the séance was held.

It is believed he wrote his first horror story, "Bernice," at the Baltimore home in 1835. It created a sensation and was considered by some readers to be "too gruesome." Poe censored his story and deleted several paragraphs, but he claimed he was giving the public what it wanted.

The furniture on the third floor room was not used by Poe, it is representative of the period.

Poe won a $50 price from the *Baltimore Sunday Visitor* newspaper for his short story, "MS Found in a Bottle."

After 1835, Poe never returned to live in Baltimore again. But he would die in the city on October 7, 1849, under mysterious circumstances, after having been found unconscious four days earlier on Lombard Street.

Halloween season at the Poe House is usually filled with special events. It is celebrated the weekend before and after Halloween.

The largest Edgar Allan Poe Birthday Celebration is held the weekend closest to the author's January 19 birth date. Special performances, exhibits and musical programs usually are part of the events.

Sources:

Edgar Allan Poe House and Museum, Commission for Historical & Architectural Preservation, Baltimore, http://www.ci.baltimore.md.us/government/historic/poehouse.html

Edgar Allan Poe Society of Baltimore, http://eapoe.org/balt/poehse.htm

Interview, Jeff Jerome, Curator, Edgar Allan Poe House, April 15, 2004

The monument and grave marker of Edgar Allan Poe in Westminster Burying Ground

R.I.P.
Edgar Allan Poe

'After the Civil War, Poe's fame exploded. Unfortunately, you couldn't see his grave because the gates were locked. In 1875, they moved him to the location near the main entrance.'—Jeff Jerome, Curator, Edgar Allan Poe House and Museum

No visit to Baltimore is complete without pausing beside the grave of Edgar Allan Poe, located in Westminster Cemetery (also called Westminster Burying Ground)—at the busy corner of Greene and Fayette streets in the heart of the city. The distinctive marble monument draws the attention of both tourists and passing locals.

On any day there's a good possibility one will find wreaths, individual flowers, bouquets and even trinkets and coins resting at the base of the noted writer's tomb.

When I stopped at the site, a single penny had been set with care inside the "O" of Poe's last name. A green plastic shamrock, and other coins, plus small handmade sprays of dried flowers, rested against the ledge at the memorial's base.

Obviously, some of the long gone visitors had come prepared. Others, seeing the tokens, had dug into their pockets or purses and joined in the custom using whatever they had at hand.

Perhaps the visitors wanted to make their presence known, to feel they had made a connection with the famous writer. They certainly felt an urge to leave something, no matter how slight or trivial, behind.

One cannot deny that there's a magic associated with Edgar Allan Poe. It begins in the early years of school, when millions of young learners are introduced to the mysterious man who wrote captivating poems and eerie stories of thumping hearts and bodies sealed behind basement walls and other themes of suspense, romance and terror.

But imagine the reaction to Poe's innovative style and controversial works during the days when they were written, when readers and proper ladies and gents in polite society were not accustomed to speaking of grave robbers and murder. It was a time when reading Poe was novel, an invitation to sneak a peek into life on the dark side—and he became a sensation.

Poe's last days

In 1849, when his career was somewhat successful, but nothing like it would become after his death, the writer stopped in Baltimore. It is believed he had been traveling on a train from Richmond to New York City.

That is when Poe mysteriously disappeared and was found in a delirious state beside a saloon on Lombard Street, in the city's Cornbeef Row area. He died four days later in Washington

This penny, left by a young Elkton boy at Poe's grave, is one of the many tributes visitors place at the site. Some believe the practice is to honor the writer, others believe it is simply to say, "I was here."

54

Medical College/Church Home and Hospital, which was closed in 2000.

Several theories have been offered as to the how and why of Poe's demise—including rabies, depression, alcoholism, drugs, an enzyme deficiency, a beating by angry potential in-laws, and murder because of unpaid debts or at the hands of Freemasons, to name a few.

Burial and reburial

Poe was interred in the Old Western Burial Ground (now known as Westminster Cemetery), but his burial plot was located in the rear of the churchyard.

His body was moved to the current location—at the corner of Greene and Fayette streets—in November 1875, 26 years after his initial burial. It is said this transfer was executed to accommodate the steady flow of admirers that wanted to visit the popular original gravesite.

During an interview for the History Channel's documentary *Haunted Baltimore,* Jeff Jerome, curator of Baltimore's Poe House and Museum, explained, "After the Civil War, Poe's fame exploded. Unfortunately, you couldn't see his grave because the gates were locked. In 1875, they moved him to the location near the main entrance. Even if the gates were locked, you could still look through the gates and still see the grave of the famous poet Edgar Allan Poe."

A gravestone with the symbol of a raven still marks Poe's original resting place. The newer,

The original grave site of Edgar Allan Poe, marked with "The Raven" tombstone, remains in the rear of the cemetery.

and more ornate and larger monument was financed in part with pennies collected from Baltimore school children.

Not surprisingly, even in death Poe has the ability to generate additional mysteries. Some conspiracy theorists claim that the author's body was stolen from its grave soon after his original burial in 1849.

Others suggest that Poe is not buried at the second gravesite because the gravediggers pulled up the wrong coffin during the exhumation in 1875.

Is it possible that the author still rests below the tomb bearing a sculpture of a solitary bird, encircled by the famous phrase, "Quoth the Raven Nevermore"?

The Poe 'Toaster'

Maybe a mysterious gravesite visitor knows the answer, but he never lingers long enough to engage in conversation.

Since 1949, every January 19 (the birth date of E.A. Poe), between the hours of midnight and 6 a.m., an unidentified visitor enters Westminster Cemetery. Jeff Jerome and a few select "grave watchers" witness the ceremonial tribute from the catacombs beneath historic Westminster Church.

A few of the simple tokens that are left behind at Poe's grave

The man, Jeff said, who is always dressed in black—except for a white scarf that covers his face—enters the churchyard and stops at the Poe grave. He then performs his annual tribute—leaving three red roses and a partially filled bottle of French cognac.

There is only speculation about the meaning of the roses and spirits. Some think the flowers are for each of the three bodies resting beneath the family plot—Edgar, his wife Virginia Clemm Poe, and his mother-in-law and aunt Maria Clemm.

No one, Jeff said, knows the special significance of the bottle of French liqueur.

There is speculation that the original "toaster," who is beginning to age, is grooming a younger man to take over responsibility to carry on the touching ritual.

But, as is appropriate with many of the stories and events related to Poe, the reasons for the customs and the identities of those involved remain a mystery.

Sources

Edgar Allan Poe House and Museum, Commission for Historical & Architectural Preservation, Baltimore, http://www.ci.baltimore.md.us/government/historic/poehouse.html

Edgar Allan Poe Society of Baltimore, http://eapoe.org/balt/poehse.htm

The Edgar Allan Poe House and Museum, brochure provided at the Poe House and Museum

Edgar Allan Poe, Wikipedia, the Free Encyclopedia, http://en.wikipedia.org/wiki/Edgar_Allan_Poe

Haunted Baltimore, The History Channel Documentary

Poe's Death, E.A. Poe Society of Baltimore, http://www.eapoe.org/geninfo/poedeath.htm

Washington Medical College http://www.springgrove.com/HistoryPics/MDHosp2.html

Who is buried in Edgar Allan Poe's Grave? http://www.usna.edu/EnglishDept/poeperplex/gravep.htm

Inteview with Jeff Jerome, Curator of the Edgar Allan Poe House and Museum, June 2004

An old vault in the dark 'catacombs' beneath Westminster Church

Touring the Westminster 'Catacombs'

'I do not see dead people, or I probably wouldn't work here.'—Lu Ann Marshall

L u Ann Marshall is a tour director, but not the type that organizes cruise ship socials and bus tours for scout troops or senior centers. It's safe to say that most people would find part of her job somewhat unusual.

"I tell people I work in a graveyard," she said, smiling as she recalled the shocked reactions her casual remark usually generates. "Then I explain it's the one where Poe is buried, and that usually stimulates the conversation."

The Baltimore native's full time responsibilities involve a bit more than lantern guided graveyard tours in one of the city's oldest cemeteries. As special project coordinator, she's also involved in events planning for the University of Maryland School of Law, which is responsible for Westminster Hall & Burying Ground.

The renovated historic church and graveyard, which contains more than 1,000 souls, is located at Fayette and Green streets in the center of town. It is best known as the burial site of Edgar Allan Poe. But the churchyard also contains the tombs of many political and military figures that played prominent roles in Maryland's early history.

A brass plate on the brick column beside the entrance near Poe's grave lists an impressive roster of "The Illustrious Men interred within this enclosure who assisted in the achievement of National Independence" during both the Revolution and War of 1812. They are at rest around and beneath the red brick church.

While one cannot help but be impressed by the achievements of generals, commodores, doctors and enlisted men, there are other stories associated with Westminster Burying Ground. But these tales have occurred in a secret place, unnoticed by tourists that walk the church's narrow public paths looking at aged granite mausoleums and weathered marble markers.

The best stories have taken place in the seclusion of an underground burial place, one hiding a number of crypts, vaults and galleries.

Usually, one thinks of these subterranean passageways in places like Rome or Mexico, where space is a premium. But beneath Westminster Hall are a number of old tombs that were dug 60 years before the church was built. Hidden from public view these graves have, over time, taken on the eerie, old-fashioned name of the "catacombs."

Standing in the dimly lit, low ceiling, dirt-floored graveyard, Lu Ann explained that the cemetery began in the late 1700s, and the church's foundation had to be constructed with care over the mausoleums and markers.

Catacomb tours are conducted on weekends from April through November. And Lu Ann has been leading them for nearly 25 years.

The archway marks the entrance to the 'catacombs.'

"There's so much history involved with this cemetery," she said. "Of course, the big attraction is Poe, but you can see the graves here of the people that many of Baltimore's streets are named after."

Listening to Lu Ann is like experiencing a talking history book. Depending upon the audience's interest, her conversation shifts from burial practices and Poe's life, to grave robbing techniques and Poe's death, then there's the War of 1812 and the numerous legends about Poe and his family.

Of course, after working for more than two decades in the burial chamber she admitted she has had her share of unusual and sometimes humorous experiences. She's also able to debunk some of the outlandish tales that have been spread but that have no substance.

"No, there have been no reports of murders, suicides or secret rituals in the catacombs," she said, firmly. "But," she added, "there have been stories of people hanging themselves in the bell tower."

When asked to comment on the presence of ghosts, she offered a less definitive answer.

"In the beginning," she said, "I always used to say 'No.' But now," she paused, looked around the large dark chamber, and said, "let me tell you a story."

It was during a Halloween weekend, she recalled, and it was quite late—around three in the morning. Lu Ann was alone, on a bench in the front section of the catacombs, where the tourists and visitors sit during a portion of her tours. Suddenly, her hair stood up and she was struck by a feeling of panic, like she had to get away from the area.

"Of course," she said, laughing at her reaction at the time, "you have to consider that I was sitting alone in a graveyard at three in the morning."

It was the first, but not the last, time that she and others would encounter strange sensations among the burial mounds beneath the church.

While filming a segment for *Scariest Places on Earth,* she said she had been up late for three nights in a row. It was about 2:30 in the morning and she was closing up the area. Again, she was on a bench when a cameraman came over and told her. "I had an odd experience, and I've worked a lot, filming these scary places. But I just had someone tap me on the back of my neck and whisper in my ear, 'Go away!' "

Lu Ann added, "It occurred in my least favorite spot in the graveyard." Then she pointed to the mausoleum of "General John Swan, 1750-1821," who had served in the Revolutionary War and who had been a friend of George Washington.

The next day, she told her colleagues in the offices, located in the old church above, and every one of them told her they had had a similar unnerving experience in the same area below.

One lady was changing one of the light bulbs in the ceiling over the catacombs when she felt someone looking at her. "That wasn't unusual," Lu Ann said, "but being tapped was. The woman said she felt very creepy and left."

On another tour, Lu Ann noticed a young man sitting in the rear pew shaking his head throughout her presentation. When she later inquired about his actions, the fellow told her that a man in a uniform kept telling him to "go away," and something was touching him on the back of his neck.

"He described the man who would be buried in that crypt," Lu Ann said, again pointing to General Swan's mausoleum.

More confirmation about the same agitating officer came from another source, a psychic representing a local ghost hunting society. Apparently the woman had been in the catacombs several times. Lu Ann said the woman announced, "Every time I come in here he tells me to 'Go away!' "

When Lu Ann asked who, the woman replied, "The commodore. He doesn't like me, but he likes my daughter."

Lu Ann Marshall stands beside a grave marker that is one of the stops on her weekend tours.

Lu Ann couldn't resist, and asked the ghost hunter, "Does he like me, because I'm in here all the time?"

Smiling, the catacomb guide was happy to relate that the general's answer (through the psychic) was "Yes."

On a different occasion, three psychics were in the benches while Lu Ann was conducting a tour, and all of the women turned their heads abruptly and at the same time. Later, they explained that they heard a small child giggling and playing peek-a-boo games.

Lu Ann said the sounds had come from the gravesite of a young girl.

From senior citizen clubs to school classes, Lu Ann has guided small groups of less than 20 to assemblies of about 100 through the labyrinth, sharing tales of history and adding a pinch of horror—just for spice.

Since Westminster Hall, located directly above, constantly hosts conferences, conventions and weddings, Lu Ann said it's quite common for her to take a handful of curious guests on a spur-of-the-moment mini-tour of the secretive and sensational burial ground.

"I've had brides and wedding parties down here for quick tours. I don't know if I'd come down here if I'd spent a thousand dollars on a gown," she said, smiling.

General Swan's mausoleum is believed to be the source of much spirited activity, which sometimes is manifested during Lu Ann's tours.

Standing in the dark atmosphere, surrounded by aged crypts and tilted tombstones with weathered letters, Lu Ann joked, "I do not see dead people, or I probably wouldn't work here. But," she rested her hand on the gravestone of Elizabeth Gunn, who died in 1806, "this is one of the spots I'm not comfortable with. I get an uneasy feeling here."

Thinking back to her early days growing up in Baltimore, near the area of the Ravens Stadium, Lu Ann said, "I was a history major in college. This job was tailor made for me. It's a great opportunity to tell people visiting Baltimore about our history and to give them a good impression of what happened here, and what we have to offer. I like to teach through interesting stories, which are both factual and entertaining."

But, not surprisingly, the conversation in the spacious sepulcher turns back to Poe. As a listener it's amazing the amount of information that Lu Ann knows about the author and what can be learned from her presentation.

"Poe is such a draw," she said. "I could stand out near his grave all day and, on a beautiful day like this, I could spend the whole time talking to people about him."

And regarding the subject of ghosts in the catacombs?

With a final smile, Lu Ann paused, then admitted, "I used to say, 'No!' that it was 'my imagination.' But now I'm not so sure."

The tall church tower overlooks the graves of many of Baltimore's most famous Colonial-era citizens.

64

For information on Westminster Hall & Burying Ground, including facilities rental, special events and catacombs tours, call (410) 706-2072.

Interesting facts

Tours of Westminster Hall & Burying Ground are scheduled for the first and third Friday (6:30 p.m.) and Saturday (10 a.m.) of each month, April through November. Reservations are required.

A Presbyterian congregation, whose members were influential in the community, purchased the graveyard property, which was originally a peach orchard, in 1786.

The Westminster Presbyterian Church was completed in 1852.

Westminster Hall is a converted Gothic church built on arches above Westminster Burying Ground, creating catacombs.

The creative restoration of the present building combined the best of the old and the new, including an 1882 Johnson pipe organ.

The hall, adjacent to the University of Maryland School of Law, is a popular setting for celebrations of all kinds. It can seat 250 for dinner and 350 in auditorium style.

Special tours of the Westminster Burying Ground and Catacombs are available year round with a minimum of 15 people.

Sources

Westminster Hall & Burying Ground, Where Baltimore's History Rests in Peace, University of Maryland School of Law publication

Westminster Hall, University of Maryland School of Law publication

Interview, Special Project Coordinator Lu Ann Marshall, Westminster Hall & Burying Ground, University of Maryland School of Law, April 29, 2004

In earlier days Fells Point was noted for shipbuilding, transportation, trade and immigration. Today, tourists flock to the popular area, which has preserved many of its historic structures—and is believed to host a number of ghosts.

Stories, Secrets and Spirits at Fells Point

'It could be that people die and want to come back to a place where they had a good time, and that's right here.'—Read Hopkins, Whistling Oyster

I n the early 1700s, the center of Baltimore was located east of today's Inner Harbor tourist area. Bars, boarding houses, brothels and boats formed a waterfront community established by the Fells, a family of merchants and shipbuilders.

Shipping and shipbuilding attracted an odd assortment of characters. They ranged from wealthy landowners and businessmen to deck hands, artisans and those who made their living serving food and drink and offering entertainment to those who were returning from or heading out to sea.

From the Revolutionary War to the Civil War era, as many as 18 shipyards operated in the Fells Point area. And while some may think the current historic district currently boasts a large number of taverns, it's worth noting there were nearly 50 saloons operating there in the late 1700s.

Area history

The village was named after William Fell, an English immigrant who founded the site between 1726-1730. Recognizing its value as a deepwater port, he began a small shipbuilding business. In the 1770s, William's son, Edward Fell, laid out the streets and gave them such English names as Thames and Shakespeare, and several exist to this day.

67

Fells Point shipbuilding increased dramatically during the American Revolution, and the industry would continue for a number of decades. During the War of 1812, more American ships were needed and the Fells Point shipyards were kept busy with orders from Congress.

When shipbuilding declined in the 1830s, the area became known as a warehousing center, handling coffee and other imports. Later, maritime steam engines overshadowed sail power, and wooden shipbuilders at Fells Point were sucked into a long downward spiral that would change their lives and livelihood.

By 1960, more than 225 years since its optimistic beginnings, the area was showing signs of urban neglect, and an expressway construction project threatened to cut through the district and destroy its buildings and its historic character.

Nearly two decades of community effort and the establishment of preservation societies enabled the neighborhood to survive, restore many of its buildings and turn Fells Point into a desirable residential neighborhood—as well as a living history center and tourist attraction.

But some believe that along the cobblestone streets and within the walls of old bars and boarding houses those who played a role in the colorful history of Fells Point have remained. Some residents and business owners believe that, at times, these souls from the past actually can make their presence known.

HAUNTS

Anyone who has read about haunted places knows there is a strong connection between restless spirits and historic buildings. If that is correct, there are probably ghost stories on every corner and in every old structure within Fells Point.

It is impossible to include a mention of every paranormal rumor and lead that surfaced during the writing of this book. Therefore, the ghost stories associated with the following sites will serve as examples of the scores of unexplained stories that are shared throughout Fells Point, a fascinating, captivating and restless historic Baltimore neighborhood.

Bertha's

Chatting with Laura Norris, owner of Bertha's, at the corner of Broadway and Lancaster Street, is an entertaining experience, mainly because the former professional violinist and present day entrepreneur has so much wonderful information to share.

From her perspective as a 30-plus-year Fells Point resident and merchant, in a few hours she was able to provide an overview of the neighborhood's 18th century founding and also explain its revitalization and resurgence as a historic site and tourist destination.

But it was ghosts that I was after, and Laura had a bagful of spirited tales to share. So she offered me the highlights of events she had heard since she and her husband, Tony, started the business in 1972.

Aware of the close connection between history and haunts, she estimated that the buildings that house her bar and restaurant were constructed about 1770-1820. She said the structures experienced a lot of traffic and spirited/lively activity, having probably served as saloons, eateries, boarding houses and mercantile establishments.

In an upstairs apartment that was rented by an artist, Laura said the tenant told a story about his cat that would freeze its motion to a halt, and the animal's fur would stand up across its back. It would remain that way and not move a muscle for an unusually long period of time.

Laura said she experienced an uneasy feeling as she passed by the site on the way to her third floor office.

"At 4 a.m., when I would close up and do my bookwork,"

Ghosts have been seen on several floors of Bertha's, and sightings have been reported by both customers and staff.

69

she said, "I would walk upstairs and say aloud, 'I'm coming through. Thanks for letting me by. Good night.' My physical body would be so entirely alive and aware. I would have goose bumps and they would go right down my spine."

In another area above the ground floor there is a spacious dance studio, with a large wall covered with mirrors.

A person doing bookwork at 6 a.m. went to the restroom and, on the way back through the dance studio saw a figure of a woman, in the mirror, dressed in black with a big hat. The worker claimed that he thought "it was an actual visage of a person." Shortly after that incident, Laura's son-in-law was in the same area of the building, about 5:30 in the morning. While coming down the stairs, he said he saw something behind him.

"When he turned around," Laura said, "he saw a male figure with a large hat and wearing a cloak, standing on the stairs."

Dee Williams, a 19-year employee at Bertha's, recalled the day her daughter brought her recently born baby into the bar. Dee, who was proud to show off her new grandchild, arranged her family visitors at a table and took several photographs.

"When I got them back," Dee recalled, "one picture had a ghostly face, and it was right on top of Shane, my grandson's, body. I showed it to my daughter and she was so upset she tore it up. She said she thought the baby was possessed. She didn't

A figure in dark clothing has been seen in the old dance studio on the second floor of Bertha's.

want to see the picture again or want anybody else to see it. I remember it looked like a shadow. I never saw anything like it."

After she ended her story, I suggested that we take a picture of Dee at the "haunted table." But I did not expect that when the photographs were developed that I would also get a ghostly image—of what appears to be a hazy face—in one of the four pictures I had taken of Dee at the spirited table. (It is not included in this chapter because it is very light and it would not reproduce at a satisfactory level.)

One morning at 3:30 a.m., a security camera monitor displayed the image of a man, inside the bar, walking back and forth.

A woman, who was upstairs in the adjoining building, was fixing a software problem on one of Laura's computers. While working, the young lady glanced at the monitor and saw a dark figure walk through the downstairs bar—long after it was closed and the building was empty.

"She said it was a big figure, really tall," Laura recalled. "The girl told herself that no one should be in the bar at that hour, and she also realized that the alarms didn't go off."

The girl left the upstairs office, went outside onto the sidewalk and peered into the street level window to try to see if she could catch a sighting of the mysterious figure. She couldn't see anything and returned upstairs to finish the work, but she said she saw the figure in the screen three times that evening.

"I figured someone had a sighting that night," Laura said.

The owner also noted there were other incidents related to the bar, such as the

This dining room table is a favorite choice of one particular ghost.

71

time when workers, who had been relaxing around 2 o'clock in the morning after the end of a long night, reported hearing footsteps in the empty rooms above them.

"They left promptly," Laura said, smiling.

A member of the waitstaff reported a sighting involving a little girl, standing or skipping and causing a rhythmic sound in a corner on the second floor.

A local paranormal group conducted an investigation, Laura said, and someone noted the spirit of a little girl, upstairs in a storeroom near a window. It's believed that the area of the sighting was once a closet, during the period when the building had been a brothel. Possibly, Laura said, the spirit of the little girl is still standing where she had been told to hide and remain by her mother, who may have been dealing with an irate customer.

"Perhaps," Laura said, "she's waiting in that long gone closet for her mother to come back, and that's why the little girl lingers."

Employee Matti Nadol mentioned the day he was working in the old dining room. An out-of-town family was having lunch, and the husband asked Matti, "Is this place haunted?"

Matti replied, "This whole neighborhood is haunted. This is the most haunted part of town."

The man seemed startled and then pointed to a nearby table, identified by the workers as Table #5. The tourist said that he saw an older man, dressed in overalls and with a beard, smoking a pipe. The man looked like a fisherman. But, when a customer walked past, the old fisherman just disappeared.

"This is a wonderful old place," Laura said. "I've never felt afraid or threatened. Of course, all buildings carry with them so much. If you're receptive, you certainly will hear or see something."

For information on Bertha's, call (410) 327-5795 or visit the web site at www.berthas.com

Cat's Eye Pub

Several persons suggested that a visit to the Cat's Eye Pub was a must, particularly to see its "Wall of Death."

The Thames Street saloon's colorfully decorated exterior and its motto, "The only thing we overlook is the harbor" made it easy to locate.

Owner Tony Cushing, who has operated the business for 30 years, admitted there are occasions when the place gets a bit spirited.

"There's a history of things falling off the walls," Tony said. "Ships, pictures, flying across the room. Sometime it seems as if they are targeting certain individuals."

Tony added that they jokingly attribute the antics to Jeff Knapp, a bartender at the pub who passed away in 1992, but who may still want to remind his old buddies of his presence.

The colorful entrance of the Cat's Eye Pub, overlooking the water

On the large wall opposite the bar, a photographic display honors a number of characters with connections to the waterfront saloon. Jeff Knapp's picture is on the wall, as is a picture of Kenny Orye, who was an owner of the Cat's Eye from 1975-1987.

"It's called the Wall of Death," Tony said, "because all the people up there have died."

While Tony didn't have any other ghost tales to tell, a few of his regular customers weren't hesitant to share their experiences in the old building. One involved former owner Kenny Orye.

The Cat's Eye Pub's "Wall of Death"

Indian Timothy, a long time regular, said he was at the bar one day when a "bartendress" was talking bad about Kenny Orye.

"I told her that wasn't right," The Indian recalled. "I told her she didn't even know Kenny. And that's when his small photograph, which was behind the bar, drops off the wall and hits her on the head."

Tony said the old building has seen its share of excitement over the years. At one time it was a biker bar, and his old partner had a strong attachment to the place.

"Kenny Orye was an old Irish biker dude," Tony said. "His spirit is definitely still hanging around."

For information on the Cat's Eye Pub, call (410) 276-9866 or visit the web site at www.catseyepub.com

Whistling Oyster

Of all the spooky sites in Fells Point, The History Channel selected the Whistling Oyster as the waterfront bar to represent this section of the city in the documentary *Haunted Baltimore*.

The Whistling Oyster's ghost stories were featured on The History Channel.

Owners Read and Louise Hopkins are proud their business is featured in the TV episode, and they admitted there was a bit of excitement associated with the filming. They also said a number of strange incidents have occurred over the years to them, to some of their customers and to their employees.

"There are spirits in this bar that are not contained in bottles,' Read said.

Read, who has operated the business for 32 years,

said the oldest part of the building dates to the 1760s. The rear room area, where we were seated for the interview next to the fireplace, was built around 1780.

Some of the early owners had slaves, Read said, but the servants lived in quarters about a block away.

Perhaps one of the slaves found a way to appear during modern times.

"One night someone in the bar saw a black man in Colonial-era attire sweeping the floor near the fireplace," Read said. "I've never seen anything, but I have heard things. People have called my name, and when I turned around there was no one there."

A few times, Read said, he has been in the bar with friends when such an incident occurred. During each occasion, both Read and his companion have heard the voice but saw no one else in the area.

A small storage closet stands against the wall between the front bar and back room. A set of stairs leading to the second floor used to stand in this area. Occasionally, Read said, people will hear phantom footsteps sounding from where the original stairs had been removed.

A story shared by Warren Newcomb, a long time Whistling Oyster employee, was recreated for The History Channel documentary. It involved an ash bucket that kept appearing in the aisle near the fireplace.

Each time Warren replaced the bucket off to the side of the room, it kept reappearing in the pathway, blocking the flow of foot traffic. Eventually, Warren said, the ash can appeared there so many times that no one wanted to touch it and put it in its proper place.

Architecturally, Read said, the Whistling Oyster

One customer said he saw a female ghost in Colonial-era clothing wiping down the bar.

offers a glimpse into the past. Some of these features are exposed original wooden beams, old-fashioned "rose nails" (created by splitting the end of an iron bar into quarters) and interior brick work, probably fashioned by Colonial-era apprentices, The long bar in the front of the establishment was put in after Prohibition. During that time, beer companies would install a saloon's bar if it carried the beer company's product. A lot of strange stories and an equal number of spirits have traveled back and forth across the top of the Whistling Oyster's bar.

Read said he was in the building one evening, after closing, talking to a bartender. "He was sitting beside me," Read recalled, "and he asked, 'Can't you see her?' When I asked what he was talking about, he said, 'The girl wiping the bar down. She's dressed in a Colonial costume and is wiping the bar down.' I didn't see anything, but that made my hair stand up on end."

Offering a possible explanation for the unusual events that have occurred at the bar, Read said, "I know a lot of people come here who haven't been in town for a long time, and they had a good time so they come back here. It could be that people die and want to come back to a place where they had a good time, and that's right here."

For information on the Whistling Oyster call (410) 342-7282.

Fell gravesite

Along Shakespeare Street, not far from the water, people

have reported seeing the figure of a man, wearing dated clothing, and they think it may be someone from a period long ago.

This finely dressed, but rather filmy apparition of a man makes his way along

The grave, located between row houses, is the resting site of several members of the Fell family, founders of Fells Point.

the narrow street, heading west, away from Broadway and then he disappears.

Some believe it is the ghost of one of the founders of Fells Point. And to many the explanation does not sound too outlandish.

On a small lot, marked by a wrought iron fence, lie the bodies of four members of the Fell family—Edward and William, Williams's son, Edward, and grandson, William. The granite marker was placed there in 1927 to mark the founder family plot.

Some believe a mansion stood nearby. But that is long gone, so too are the shipyards and slaves, the clipper ships and wooden hulled warships.

But the memories of the Fells—and the sailors and sweethearts, immigrants and craftsmen, harlots and merchants—and all who worked at Fells Point before it became the tourist destination it is today, well, maybe a few of them have remained. And, just like the spirits of the Fells, they too may take quiet walks along the streets on lonely nights, recalling days long gone by.

For information on Fells Point events and history, contact The Preservation Society, at (410) 675-6750 or visit its web site at www.preservationsociety.com, which also conducts a ghost walk.

For information on the Original Fells Point Ghost Tours, visit www.fellspointghost.com

Interesting facts

Around the year 1730, Englishman William Fell purchased the land that would become Fells Point, seeing its potential as a shipbuilding and shipping port. Originally, it was called Long Island Point. Later, the name was changed to Fells Point.

In 1773, Baltimore annexed Fells Point, but when shipping and warehousing moved up river to the Inner Harbor area, shipbuilding continued to thrive in the Fells Point area of the city.

Many ship captains and ship owners lived in the two-and-a-half-story houses in Fells Point, some of which have been restored.

The *Hornet* and *Wasp*, the first two ships of the American Navy, were commissioned at Fells Point.

Fells Point is considered the birthplace of the frigate USS *Constellation*, launched in 1797.

By the end of the Revolutionary War in 1783, nearly 250 privateers had sailed from Baltimore and many of these ships that harassed British vessels were built in Fells Point.

By the period of the War of 1812, Fells Point shipbuilders had established themselves with the creation of the Baltimore Clipper, a trade ship known for its handling and speed.

Nearly 130 privateers operated out of Baltimore during the War of 1812, capturing more than 500 British ships.

Until 1850, Fells Point was Baltimore's point of entry for European immigrants.

When the center of Baltimore's maritime commerce shifted to the Inner Harbor area after the Civil War, Fells Point was still known as "Sailor Town" and its businesses and services catered to seamen arriving and departing from the city.

In 1969, Fells Point was named the first National Registered Historic District in Maryland.

Years ago, some people believed the grave on Shakespeare Street contained the remains of the famous English bard, William Shakespeare. A granite marker, placed at the site in 1927, solved that mystery. The stone states that the small plot, located between 1605 and 1609 Shakespeare Street, is the resting place of Fell family members.

For several years, filming of the popular television series *Homicide*, which was set in Baltimore, took place in the area. A large brick city building, located on the harbor on Thames Street, served as the TV detectives' office.

Tourists and residents have reported seeing apparitions walking along the narrow streets of Fells Point.

Sources:

"Baltimore: A Maritime History, Shipbuilding—Fells Point," http://www.columbia.edu/als209/assign2/shipbuilding.html

Randy Dunkle, "Fells Point, Tales From Charm City: The Ghosts of Fells Point," http://www.baltimorestories.com/_fp/fp_rd_ghost.html

Brennen Jensen, "Mobtown Beat, Charmed Life: Point, Counter Point," *Baltimore City Paper*, October 16-22, 2002

Maryland Ghost & Spirit Association, http://www.marylandghosts.com/locations/baltimorecity.shtml

Haunted Baltimore, The History Channel Documentary

"Neighborhood History: History of Fells Point," http://livebaltimore.com/history/fellspnt.html

The Preservation Society. Saving the past for the future, http://www.preservationsociety.com/fellspointwalkngtours2003.html

Interview, Laura Norris, Bertha's, March 30, 2004

Interview, Read Hopkins, Whistling Oyster, March 30, 2004

Interview, Tony Cushing, Cat's Eye Pub, April 8, 2004

Bertha's

Cat's Eye Pub

Whistling Oyster

Fell's Gravesite

Shakespeare Street

A Baltimore version of the "Vanishing Hitchhiker" folktale refers to a young girl named Sequin, whose ghost appears along Route 40.

East Baltimore's Very Own 'Vanishing Hitchhiker'

'The ghost tale involving the vanishing hitchhiker
"is probably the most popular ghost story still in circu-
lation today." '—Jane Yolen

According to storyteller and author Jane Yolen, America has many spooky stories and legends of the unexplained that are associated with particular locales. However, the ghost tale involving the vanishing hitchhiker "is probably the most popular ghost story still in circulation today."

The urban legend expert Jan Harold Brunvand, author of several books on folklore including one entitled *The Vanishing Hitchhiker*, said settings for the often-told tale are international. He added that the story's supernatural twist has made it one of the most popular tales told in settings throughout the world.

The mysterious hitchhiker is a man or woman, who accepts a ride from a stranger, and the vehicle has been a horse, buggy, automobile, delivery truck or tractor-trailer.

Other elements of the mysterious tale have involved a young ghost, a nearby cemetery, an article of clothing and, at times, a special name that over the years remains associated with the story and, as a result, relates the version to a particular setting.

In our Baltimore account, the mysterious maiden is named "Sequin." Her story takes place along Route 40, and it offers many of the classic elements of the well-known and often repeated legend.

Old Route 40 begins at the Atlantic Ocean and ends in the mountains of Utah. It's a famous road, the nation's first intercontinental highway. It leaves the beach sand and passes through farmland, over rivers and train tracks, through small towns, and villages and major cities—including Baltimore.

At the very least, tens of thousands of stories can be told by the residents who live along this major roadway or work in small shops beside its east-west traffic lanes. But one Baltimore tale bears repeating, even though its variations can be heard in every state in the union, whether there is any connection to Route 40 or not.

For many years, stories have circulated about a young, attractive, blonde girl who appears at times along Route 40 wearing a low-cut, blue sequined cocktail dress. It's not specific whether the story takes place within or just outside of the east end of the city, and no one knows for sure how much is true and how much is simply the result of fertile imaginations.

But it doesn't matter. Regardless of its origin, it remains a good story.

Many years ago—no one knows exactly when—a Sunday school teacher used to tell his classes about a young girl with violet eyes and blonde hair. Apparently, the girl used to wait outside the church to meet the boys from his class when their lessons were completed.

Over time, it's believed that she dated every one of the boys, and people in the area began describing the girl as "immoral."

One Sunday, after the church services were over, the blonde headed girl was seated in the back of the church. Some say she was there because the pastor was giving away clothes that had been donated by members of the nearby community and his church.

When the pastor opened one of the boxes and pulled out a flimsy, blue sequined party dress, the girl ran down the center aisle, grabbed the fancy garment and rushed out of the church.

After that incident, the girl was always seen wearing the blue cocktail style dress, no matter what the occasion, time of day or condition of the weather.

That winter the weather was brutal. The Sunday school teacher was shocked to learn that the young girl was discovered dead in the snow, and she was wearing only the blue, light-weight dress. Everyone said she had frozen to death.

Occasionally, after her funeral, people in the neighborhood reported sightings of the deceased girl, and the apparitions usually occurred late in the evening along Route 40. But not too many people believed the rumors. After all, anyone with an ounce of sense knew that such an event was impossible.

Several years later, two local college students were driving along Route 40 heading to a dance. They said they saw a pretty girl standing on a corner wearing a blue cocktail dress.

They pulled over to the corner, talked to her for a while and invited her to come with them for the evening. She agreed and she and the boys had a wonderful time. She told them that her name was Sequin.

On the ride home to east Baltimore, the girl, who was in the back seat, said she was cold. One of the boys gave her his long tan overcoat.

When they arrived at her address, she got out of the car, raced up the steps, waved good-bye and disappeared into her house.

The next day, when the boy realized he had not gotten his coat, the two friends drove to the girl's home.

A clue to the mystery of the vanishing girl was left atop a lonely grave.

An elderly woman answered the door. When the boys said they were looking for Sequin, the woman frowned, shook her heard and replied, "This is rather strange. You two must be old friends of hers. You see, she's been dead for 10 years."

Shocked, the boys thought they had come to the wrong house, but the woman assured them that they were at the right place. "They found her exactly 10 years ago, last night. I thought someone would be coming here today. I get a visitor each year around the anniversary of her departure."

She explained that Sequin was her daughter's nickname. Everyone called her that because she always worn the same blue cocktail dress. The woman said her daughter's real name was Molly, and then she shared the story of how the girl was found, near Route 40, frozen to death.

The mother gave the boys directions to the girl's grave. "It's one of the larger stones, and it has the most beautiful carved angel on top of it," she said, beginning to cry. "We chose an angel because that's what my Molly, my little girl, was to me. She was a precious little, kind and soft angel. Never hurt anyone. She was just confused. Lived in a world of her own, poor little thing. But it hurts me that she's still not at peace, that she still has that restless side, even after all this time."

The boys thought the old woman was crazy, but they had time to kill and decided to check out her strange story. They drove to the cemetery, followed the directions and after a bit of searching located Molly's gravesite.

Hanging from the girl's worn marker, and draped over the top of the pitted stone and beneath the tall angel, was the missing overcoat that the young boy had loaned to Sequin the night before.

Sources

Jan Harold Brunvand, "The Vanishing Hitchhiker," *Encyclopedia of Urban Legends*, W.W. Norton & Co.

Josephine Novak, "A Pretty Hitchhiker Called Sequin," *The Evening Sun*, Oct. 25, 1976

Jane Yolen, "A Pretty Girl in the Road," *Favorite Folktales From Around the World*, Pantheon Books

This hill, in the old German cemetery beside O'Donnell Heights, could have been one of the roads used by the elusive "Phantom" during the summer of terror in 1951.

Ed Okonowicz

Phantom of O'Donnell Heights

'It was just after midnight yesterday morning and throughout the project people waited—in nervous groups on porches and behind drawn shades—for the phantom to strike.'—*The Sun,* July 25, 1951

T he Garden State has its Jersey Devil, plus an assortment of aliens who visited during the *War of the Worlds.* The American Northwest proudly claims Sasquatch, and the nearby Chesapeake Bay is home of Chessie, the elusive sea serpent. But in the summer of 1951, Baltimore had its own crazed creature, one that terrorized the O'Donnell Heights neighborhood and then vanished as mysteriously and as suddenly as it had arrived.

As the story goes, for several weeks residents of the row house neighborhood on the east side of the city reported that a strange presence was terrorizing their community.

Based on newspaper accounts, the object of concern was not your run-of-the-mill, basic burglar or prowler. Instead, this "phantom," as it was named, possessed supernatural powers that allowed it to leap from 20-foot-tall buildings and jump over six-foot-high, barb-wire-topped cemetery fences with apparent ease.

The fiend was described as wearing black robes and lurking at night in search of its prey. Break-ins, family disturbances, teenager mischief and just about anything out of the ordinary was attributed to the phantom.

In a July 25, 1951 article in *The Sun*, the reporter shared comments from the dozen residents he had interviewed. His article captured the bedlam that the mysterious visitor had created, the attention it attracted throughout the city and the reason it received front-page attention.

The writer reported the scene, just after midnight, when "throughout the project people waited—in nervous groups on porches and behind drawn shades—for the phantom to strike." One man kept lookout, while resting atop a garbage can, with his .12 gauge shotgun for protection.

Other weapons reportedly held at the ready by residents of the neighborhood under attack included pipes, clubs, baseball bats and butcher knives.

A woman complained that her husband, who had been on watch so many nights for the creature, was suffering because his "eyeballs ache from staying awake so long."

Another man announced that after the black, cape clad phantom had jumped off a roof, he and friends "chased him down into the graveyard."

Many folks believed the phantom dwelled in one of the old graveyards surrounding the community. There are frequent reports of residents chasing the phantom up "Cemetery Hill" and "Graveyard Hill."

There was a claim that the phantom was seen "under that big sarcophagus" and one resident swore the creature "went back to his grave."

Several cemeteries, including Mount Carmel Cemetery, Oheb Shalom Cemetery, the German Cemetery (Gottesacker, Der Ersted, The First God's Field) and St. Stanislaus Cemetery surround the community and are within

Mount Carmel Cemetery is located across the road from O'Donnell Heights.

88

a simple leap and bound for the elusive beast.

Eventually, every barking dog and mischievous incident was blamed on the phantom. Police, who were patrolling the neighborhood in search of the creature, began arresting youngsters who were hiding in graveyards and blaming the phantom for their actions.

Also, self-appointed bounty hunters from other parts of the city were patrolling the area's streets, attempting to snare the specter and get their names in the newspaper. Even a pipe, sticking up from a roof, had been thought to be the elusive creature of the night.

No one knows who or what the O'Donnell Heights Phantom was, or where the black-robed wraith went. But there were plenty of opinions

This impressive sculpture is at the entrance of St. Stanislaus Cemetery, a large graveyard adjacent to O'Donnell Heights.

and a lot of sleepless nights in the summer of 1951, in the east Baltimore neighborhood surrounded by graveyards.

Sources

Tom Chalkley, Charles Cohen, Brennen Jensen, "Baltimore's Ghost Stories to Tingle Your Spine," *Baltimore City Paper online*, Oct. 25-31, 2000

John Sherwood, "A Neighborhood Legend, When the Phantom Roamed," *Evening Sun*, February 28, 1962

"Fear In The Night, Phantom Prowler Terrorizes O'Donnell Heights Residents," *The Sun*, July 25, 1951

Black Aggie's original pedestal, minus the infamous statue, as it currently appears in the Agnus family plot in Pikesville's Druid Ridge Cemetery

Black Aggie . . . Baltimore's Long Lasting Legend

'Some very prominent citizens come up and share some of the high jinx they pulled years ago.'—Beau Reid, Family Services Counselor, Druid Ridge Cemetery

Glowing red eyes in a graveyard at midnight. Pregnant women cursed with stillborn babies. Fraternity initiation rites conducted amongst tombstones beneath a full moon. Mobs of midnight visitors. A pirated statue design. At least one young man who was scared to death and found lying beneath its shadow. And a missing metal arm.

These are only a few of the many bizarre stories and legends that have been associated with Baltimore's "Black Aggie," a rather gloomy looking, shrouded sculpture that has achieved icon status. And although more than 35 years have passed since this mysterious monument was hauled from its cemetery pedestal, riveting tales of terror persist and a steady stream of curious visitors still comes to call.

History

Our rather strange story begins at the turn of the 20th century. That's when *Baltimore American* publisher Felix Agnus, a prominent Baltimore citizen who had served as a Union general during the Civil War, purchased an artwork to mark his family plot in Druid Ridge Cemetery, located in Pikesville, just outside the city limits.

The eerie figure—installed at the graveyard atop a stone platform bearing the AGNUS family name—was a knock-off

91

reproduction of a piece of artwork that had been created by noted sculptor Augustus Saint-Gaudens.

The original piece had been commissioned by historian Henry Adams, a descendant of the Adams family—he was the grandson of U.S. President John Quincy Adams (#6) and great-grandson of Declaration of Independence signer and U.S. President John Adams (#2).

The stunning, yet depressing piece—unofficially named "Grief" by some observers—had been erected in Washington's Rock Creek Cemetery as a memorial to Henry Adams' wife Marian, who died while only in her 40s.

Apparently, someone made a casting of the original work, and the life-size imitation was accepted by publisher Agnus as the perfect figure to adorn his family plot and honor his deceased wife, Annie Agnus. In 1907, the copy of the original creation was placed on its granite base outside Baltimore and a storm of controversy erupted over the appropriateness of owning and displaying the unsanctioned copy of the original.

Members of the Adams and Saint-Gaudens families protested the Agnus cemetery sculpture, and lawsuits were initiated. Saint-Gaudens' widow wanted the statue removed. Felix Agnus was adamant that his version of the monument remain at his Pikesville family plot. Agnus' argument against the suit was successful and "Grief's" residence seemed secure. She remained perched at the top of a rolling hillside among granite crosses, carved angels and thousands of less distinctive markers bearing names sculpted in stone.

Haunts and legends

Initially, the Agnus Memorial did not attract much attention, but in the midst of the era known as the Roaring Twenties, for a reason we will never discover, the sculpture seemed to develop its own personality. Some might even say, it took on a diabolical life of its own.

It was shortly after Felix Agnus' death (on Halloween, Oct. 31, 1925) that the Baltimore legend was born. The contemplative and curious looking creature seemed to awaken from its slumber and earned its very special name "BLACK AGGIE."

For more than 40 years, from the 1920s through the 1960s, the area surrounding the eerie metal creation became a must-visit site for daytime passers-by and late evening adventurers.

During weekend afternoons, slow moving processions of automobiles bearing locals and tourists would drive the narrow lanes of Druid Ridge Cemetery, pausing to take photographs of Black Aggie that later were shown off to friends and neighbors. When darkness fell, however, less mannerly explorers arrived on foot, making secretive, unofficial pilgrimages to the "sinister" statue.

College fraternities decided Black Aggie would be an excellent assistant to evaluate applicants. As part of their initiation rites, hopefuls were ordered to sit in Black Aggie's lap to prove they were worthy of membership. One folktale claims that a young man died from a heart attack while in the statue's clutches, and in the morning workmen discovered the body beside Black Aggie's feet.

Naturally, more stories and tales traveled through the friend-of-a-friend message chain, and the bizarre but interesting accounts combined to establish the statue's status as Baltimore's premier urban legend.

Some said that even walking beneath the creature's shadow would have dire consequences.

Pregnant mothers claimed to experience miscarriages, and others told stories that no vegetation or flora would grow in the shade of Aggie's ominous figure. (Perhaps the latter was due to the constant traffic around the gravesite that destroyed grass and plantings that had to continually be replaced.)

Those unsure of where Black Aggie held court would only have to enter the cemetery and wait until the stoke of midnight, for it was at the bewitching hour

Vandalism, in the form of graffiti, carved into the likeness of General Felix Agnus, on his tombstone

93

when two bright red dots would appear. To no one's surprise, these were the bristling fires of hell glowing from the statue's demonic eyes.

As legends associated with Black Aggie grew more bizarre, visits by couples and groups were more numerous, and midnight escapades by crowds swelled in size and multiplied in frequency. Beneath the shrouded figure, young women lost their virginity, drunken parties were held and wicked rituals were conducted.

One story surfaced that in 1962 a workman found one of Black Aggie's arms, which had been cut off the night before. Another tale reported that the statue was the likeness of an area nurse who was hung, in error, for an unstated crime. Those responsible were said to have bought the statue as a penance to atone for their mistake and the accompanying guilt.

By the 1960s, vandalism from unauthorized nighttime visits and the legend's growing notoriety became serious disruptions to the operation, maintenance and reputation of the peaceful country-style cemetery

It will never be known how many fraternity initiates sat on Black Aggie's lap, felt the heat from her hands and then jumped away at the last moment to avoid being crushed by the monster's grip. And we can only estimate the number of Baltimoreans who made unofficial pilgrimages to catch a glimpse of the eerie edifice in action.

But there is no doubt that the numbers are substantial.

Eventually, the staff decided it could no longer handle the spell that Black Aggie had cast over multiple generations of Baltimore area residents and thrill seekers. To help solve these growing problems, Agnus family descendants decided to remove the statue aptly named "Grief," which was causing much of the same.

Everyone has a story

Beau Reid is a lifelong Baltimore resident and currently works as a family services counselor at Druid Ridge Cemetery. One spring morning he escorted me to the site of the Agnus plot, located in the Annandale section, one of the oldest portions of the picturesque graveyard that opened in 1896.

Although Black Aggie is gone, we stood beside the monument where the monster used to hold court. Shaking his head,

Reid said, "We get three or four calls a month about her, from people who want to come up and see where she used to be or to find out some information. We're constantly guiding people up here. They want to know the story and also ask how long she's been gone."

Reid said that if 20 or more people visit the cemetery for a service, several who happen to be in the 45- to 60-year-old age range will mention Black Aggie and ask for directions to the Agnus grave.

"Some very prominent citizens come up and share some of the high jinx they pulled years ago," Reid said, smiling.

While speaking to Jeff Jerome, curator of the Edgar Allan Poe House, Black Aggie's name came up in conversation. Immediately, the prominent Baltimore historian smiled and recalled the evening he and a young lady made a pilgrimage along the dark lanes of Druid Ridge Cemetery.

"I'm one of the thousands that went to Druid Ridge," Jeff said. "I was there with a date. It was Halloween night. We decided to go. We were young. It was dark. Eventually, we saw a high beam of light, and a caretaker shouted out, 'Turn around right now!' That's the closest we got to Black Aggie that night."

He added that he has seen pictures of people sitting proudly in Black Aggie's lap. "It's amazing, even though she's been gone a long time, people still make the trip to Druid Ridge, and people still share their stories about Black Aggie."

Lu Ann Marshall, tour director at Westminster Hall and Burying Ground, site of the Poe grave and church catacombs, grinned at the mention of Black Aggie. A Baltimore native, Lu Ann was eager to share her memories of the legendary statue.

"As a kid," she said, "I remember putting my head under my pillow and saying 'Black Aggie' three times. It was said that if you did that she would appear under your bed, and that if you touched her she would scare you to death. I was terrified. I also remember that they said if you laid in her arms you would die."

Then Lu Ann added, "She's gone you know."

When I replied that I was heading off to take Aggie's photograph at her present residence, Lu Ann, like others to whom I had talked, became excited and asked for a copy of the legend's picture.

Black Aggie on display

Thanks to very helpful and specific directions provided by Wayne Schaumburg, Baltimore historian and noted tour guide at Green Mount Cemetery, I caught up with Black Aggie in Washington, D.C., only a block from the White House.

In 1967, after she was hauled off her granite podium, Black Aggie was acquired (depending upon which source you discover) either by the Maryland Institute of Art or the Smithsonian American Art Museum or the National Collection of Fine Arts or the National Museum of American Art. While she may have been displayed temporarily, most sources agree that for several years she was relegated to a dark corner beneath a stairwell in a museum basement.

In about 1987, the mystifying sculpture was transferred to the General Services Administration, which placed her on display in the courtyard of the Federal Judicial Center, located across from Lafayette Square, adjacent to the Dolley Madison House.

Through a red brick, gated archway, with a brass plate proclaiming "Entrance to 717 Madison Place," the Baltimore icon sits alone, beneath a street lamp and surrounded by shrubbery. Her veiled face gives the impression she is asleep, inactive and benign. Each day, she is ignored, or at most glanced at, by federal workers who eat their lunch and chat casually at round picnic

Black Aggie, at rest in the Madison Place courtyard, beside the Dolley Madison House in Washington, D.C., only a block from The White House

tables. Tourists carrying cameras and guide maps pass by, unfazed and unimpressed by the quiet, green-gray creature that seems at peace in the manicured garden.

None of the workers or visitors has any idea that in their midst sits a creature that had once achieved a horrifying celebrity status in her hometown.

And who would have imagined that more than 35 years since her departure from her Baltimore abode, just a passing mention of the words "Black Aggie" still has the power to delight, entertain and, in some cases, even terrify?

Sources:

Black Aggie,
http://groups.msn.com/MarylandtheoldSupernaturalStompingGround/the
historyofblackaggie.msnw

Black Aggie, Pikesville's Ghostly Statue,
http://www.baltimoremd.com/content/blackaggie.html

Catherine Mezensky, "Monumentally Speaking, Black Aggie Baltimore's Most Mysterious Statue," *The Urbanite Magazine*, February 2001

Druid Ridge Cemetery, http://thebrgs.homestead.com/druidridge-ns4.html

Massachusetts Historical Society, www.masshist.org

Troy Taylor, "Haunted Maryland, Black Aggie of Druid Ridge Cemetery," Ghosts of the Prairie, http://www.prarieghosts.com/druidridge.html

Interview, Wayne R. Schaumburg, Green Mount Cemetery, April 8, 2004

Interview, Beau Reid, Druid Ridge Cemetery, April 15, 2004

Interview, Jeff Jerome, Edgar Allan Poe House, April 15, 2004

Interview, Lu Ann Marshall, Westminster Hall, April 29, 2004

Field Visit, Dolley Madison House, May 3, 2004

The Booth Family plot, which holds the body of assassin John Wilkes Booth, is one of the most popular locations in Green Mount Cemetery.

City Stories
Carved in Stone

'Green Mount reflects how those who lived in the Victorian period dealt with death. This is a parklike setting where people would come on a Sunday after noon to stroll among the monuments. They would admire the artwork and have a picnic as they sat beside Aunt Mary's grave.' —Wayne Schaumburg

W hen most people need to solve one of history's minor or major puzzles, they usually scour library special collections, historical society and state archives, genealogical documents, courthouse records and the massive amount of Internet information available with a quick click of their trusty mouse.

But there's a different approach that offers clues and solutions to some of history's mysteries in a rather unusual setting— making a visit to your local cemetery.

Whether you live in an urban center or in a rural village, in a suburban development or in a forgotten historic town, cemeteries can provide a fair number of answers, and also present a lot of new questions. And the added bonus is that a graveyard search is just plain fun.

Anyone who wants to know just how enjoyable a cemetery excursion can be need only inquire of Wayne Schaumburg. The 57-year-old Baltimore native is an historian and a schoolteacher who spends a fair amount of his spare time walking among the dead.

For nearly two decades, beginning in the first few weeks of spring, Wayne steps briskly along tree lined paths bordered by stone obelisks, granite sculpted shrouds and simple marble markers.

His excursions take place in Green Mount Cemetery, a 68-acre rectangular patch of earth located in the center of town. Over the last 20 years, the Baltimore boneyard has become Wayne's domain.

On a chilly and overcast April morning, a month before his annual spring public tours began, I was treated to a private walk through Green Mount. Smiling like a pitcher arriving at spring training camp, Baltimore's noted graveyard historian was obviously pleased. The time had finally arrived for him to prepare for the pilgrims who would be coming to hear about the lives and deaths of his city's rich, famous and infamous.

With camera and paper and pen in hand, I raced to keep up with my host, who led with a vigorous step, talking along the way. Pausing at select cemetery sites over the remains of long silent notables, Wayne told tales and shared stories of who's who and who was of Baltimore.

Moving from the eternal resting sites of such well known Baltimore names as Walters and Pratt, Hopkins and Rinehart, Wayne offered an enticing verbal blend of humor and history, art and architecture, rumor and romance—and, of course, an unsolved mystery or two.

A sculpture created by the talented artist W. H. Rinehart

After giving the spring tours for so many years, Wayne knew what I wanted to see and he also knew most of the questions I was going to ask.

For starters, he directed me to the John Wilkes Booth's gravesite, which was at the top of my wish list.

The Booth plot

"This is the most asked about grave in the cemetery," Wayne said, placing his hand against the tall, white obelisk bearing the family name BOOTH in block letters. "People get excited about it," he added, pointing to the infamous name of the assassin that is listed on the back of the tall stone.

Wayne explained that the name, "John Wilkes"—carved amidst several other members of his family—is the only indication that Abraham Lincoln's murderer is located in the Booth plot. ("Plot" as in area of ground, of course. One has to be careful to explain the precise meaning when using the words "Booth" and "plot" in the same sentence.)

But questions about how the murderer's corpse eventually arrived in Baltimore presented Wayne with an opportunity to share one of his many fascinating tales.

In 1869, Wayne explained, Edwin, the actor and John's brother, was able to arrange for the release of the assassin's body, which had been buried—along with the other conspirators—in the grounds of the Washington Penitentiary.

The Booth family was from nearby Harford County, Maryland, and Edwin wanted his brother brought home. He had no

John Wilkes Booth's name appears on this family stone, but there is no marker that indicates his exact burial site.

interest, Wayne said, in turning the gravesite into a Confederate shrine or allowing the family plot to become a site that Union loyalists would desecrate. Therefore, there is no specific marker that designates precisely where John Wilkes is buried.

When President Andrew Johnson signed a document allowing for release of the body to the family, the killer's corpse arrived in a simple coffin in Baltimore in February 1869. Because it was the middle of winter, the ground was too hard for the grave to be opened, so the body was stored in a holding vault at Green Mount until late June.

It's written that the burial ceremony was an eerie affair— held in the evening, with lit torches used for illumination—and attended by Booth family members and a few friends.

Smiling, Wayne pointed out that the old saying "No good deed goes unpunished" applied to a helpful clergyman who recited comforting passages at the assassin's graveside service.

To no one's surprise, Wayne said, there was no religious person in the area who was willing to speak at John Wilkes' requiem. Somehow, the Booth family engaged the spiritual talents of Rev. Fleming James, an Episcopal minister from New York, who, some say, was visiting friends in the city.

It is not known if the helpful reverend was informed that the deceased was the notorious murderer of the late great president of the United States, or if the preacher assumed he was lending a helping hand to an average family in need. Nevertheless, when his congregation in New York discovered that their very own Rev. James had officiated at the ceremony of John Wilkes Booth, they dismissed the well-intentioned padre from his position as leader of their flock.

"There are stories," Wayne said, with a noticeable pause, "that John Wilkes Booth is not really here. That he was never caught and that he escaped to the mid-West and died at a very old age. Others say he was buried in Virginia."

Apparently, the conspiracy theories about Booth persist to this day, Wayne said, adding that a court case 10 years ago involved a petition to exhume John Wilkes Booth's corpse and test its DNA to see if Lincoln's assassin really rests in Green Mount.

The court denied the request, Wayne said, and the cemetery board probably was quite relieved with the decision, especially since a full-scale media circus would have accompanied the exhumation process and testing procedures.

A country estate

After climbing to the ridge of a hill on the south side of the cemetery, Wayne pointed across at the sloping terrain, accented with mausoleums, monuments and memorials of all shapes and sizes.

"This is an example of an urban-rural cemetery," Wayne said. "It opened in 1839. And for anybody who was anybody in Baltimore, who died between 1850 and 1950, this became the place to be buried. "

He said the cemetery is "a parklike setting that was built just on the edge of town," which at the time was rural and completely different than the way area looks today.

Originally, the land was the country estate of Robert Oliver, a successful merchant, who made his money, Wayne said, "with fast ships and quick wits."

The cemetery founders purchased more than half of the 107-acres of Oliver's country getaway and established a resting place

The main entrance to Green Mount Cemetery presents a castle-like appearance. The spacious city graveyard hosts Baltimore's rich and famous and is surrounded by tall stone walls.

that was much more spacious than the crowded graveyards located in small lots beside churches in the older sections of the city.

The resting place of approximately 68,000 souls is surrounded by an impressive stone wall that originally was used to mark the border of the graveyard. Today, locked gates and additions that have made the wall taller keep out those who would vandalize the architectural treasures that have been preserved since the days before the Civil War.

While pointing out the interesting tombstones and notable residents, Wayne added that people seeking interesting epitaphs usually are disappointed. "By the time it opened, the era of the catchy epitaph was passé. But," he said, "Green Mount reflects how those who lived in the Victorian period dealt with death. This is a parklike setting—a Victorian pleasure garden to mask the ugliness of death—where people would come on a Sunday afternoon to stroll among the monuments. They would admire the artwork and have a picnic as they sat beside Aunt Mary's grave. The people here were considered to be in a resting or sleeping state."

One can imagine, Wayne said, all of the other funereal practices and objects associated with death during that period— mourning clothes, family and religious customs, even special jewelry and stationery. All of this, he added, is reflected in the tombstone architecture and it offers a glimpse of the attitude of the time.

The rich and famous

Continuing our walk, Wayne pointed to the headstone of Allen Welsh Dulles, a director of the Central Intelligence Agency. "I mention that his grave is bugged," Wayne said, with a grin, then added, "in more ways than one."

He pointed to the stone of noted photographer A. Aubrey Bodine, whose work, primarily in black-and-white, appeared in the *Baltimore Sun's Sunday Sun Magazine* and several national publications. Bodine's grave marker features a camera lens and a representation of the photographer's signature.

Overlooking an area known as the Rose Circle, Wayne said, "We almost got the Duke and Duchess of Windsor," then explained how Edward, the man who would have been king of

England, and his wife, Baltimore native Wallis Warfield Simpson, bought a plot in Green Mount when the royal couple thought they would not be allowed entry into England's Frogmore in Windsor Park. After Queen Elizabeth II eventually granted the couple permission to enter the royals' official burial site, the duke and duchess gave up their Green Mount plot.

Sixteen Civil War generals and one Civil War admiral are buried in Green Mount, including Joseph E. Johnston, a major figure in the Southern command. Wayne said there are more Confederate generals than Union in the cemetery.

After passing the graves of Johns Hopkins (Johns was the family name of his grandmother), and Enoch Pratt (as in the city library), we stopped at an ornate sarcophagus that was shielded entirely by a large plastic-like covering.

That is how the marvelously carved tombstone of Arunah S. Abell, founder of the *Baltimore Sun*, has been protected from vandalism and preserved from environmental assault. Created by stone carver Hugh Sisson, Wayne described the work as "magnificent," which is accented with ornate lettering and delicate flowers whose detail looks as fresh as when the artwork was set in place.

A signature and a camera lens mark the resting place of this famous Baltimore photographer.

Walking toward a few unusual markers—including a dark, meteor-like stone (which remains a mystery) and a bathtub-shaped monument (complete with drain hole)—Wayne said Green Mount is home to Maryland's governors and Baltimore's mayors, business leaders, philanthropists, artists, authors and numerous notables.

"I've been doing this tour for nearly 20 years," Wayne said, "and I am amazed at the new things I discover whenever I visit."

While his normal tour focuses on selected famous people and their stories, my guide said he could develop additional tours that would simply spotlight the cemetery's architecture, tombstone symbolism or works or art. (There are almost a dozen bronze sculptures on the grounds.)

Visitors from near and far

The gravesite of John Walter Lord, author of *A Night to Remember*, about the sinking of the *Titanic*, is another popular site, as is the resting place of poet Sidney Lanier.

"We get people from all over the country on our tours," Wayne said, "and they come for a variety of reasons. Some have a passing interest in cemeteries and others are aficionados."

Many were Baltimore residents who come back to the city because they had never visited Green Mount, others stop at the graves of relatives, some are Civil War enthusiasts and others have specific interest in a particular person.

Wayne mentioned a Georgia couple that had gone to visit every site associated with poet Sidney Lanier. They took trips to places where he wrote, where he worked and where he lived.

"But they had never seen his burial site,"

A small section of Green Mount Cemetery, which displays a wide range of funereal architecture

106

Wayne said, recalling the emotional nature of their visit. "When I took them to the grave, it was like they had discovered Valhalla."

"Green Mount is the story of Baltimore, and it is the story of burial practices from 1840 to the present. You mention a type of monument or burial practice and it's here. This is a Baltimore treasure," Wayne said, "and the officials at Green Mount take great effort to see that it is preserved."

After nearly two decades, Wayne said, the tours and the experiences associated with his work have never become boring.

"I look forward to it," he said, "talking about the history. Baltimore has a lot of history that people don't know. Pratt, Walters, Hopkins, they're all here. Talking about their lives and what they did, and getting to know the people who come on the tours, is very satisfying."

For information on the regularly scheduled spring and fall tours of Green Mount Cemetery, visit Wayne's web site at http://home.earthlink.net/~wschaumburg or send him an e-mail at wschaumburg@earthlink.net or call him at (410) 256-2180.

Sources:

Jacques Kelly, "Grave issues of some note," *The Baltimore Sun*, May 27, 1996

Jackie Nickel, "Cemetery tours bring famous Baltimoreans back to life," *Avenue News*, Oct. 31, 2001

Frederick N. Rasmussen, "Booth's fate was both fame and obscurity," *The Baltimore Sun*, April 12, 2003

Frederick N. Rasmussen, "Windsors had a plot at Green Mount," *The Baltimore Sun*, April 29, 1986

Jane Sellman, "Haunted Places in Baltimore," http://www.baltimore.to/Guide/baltimore_haunted_places.html

Green Mount Cemetery document, "List of Marked Grave Sites— Numbered"

Interview, Wayne R. Schaumburg, Green Mount Cemetery, April 8, 2004

The ghost said to haunt the Baltimore Theatre Project has been described as a talented musician.

Mysterious Musician on West Preston Street

'No one was ever terrified or frightened. They would just ask, "Who was that guy?" They may have thought it was peculiar, but no one was ever scared.'
—Robert Mrozek, Theatre Project Producing Director, 1990-2001

Take an old, 19th-century building that originally housed a men's fraternal organization, add a theater group featuring dynamic and experimental productions and toss in a restless presence that seems drawn to perform on the building's piano and you've got the makings of an unusual story that features a talented and friendly ghost.

On West Preston Street, several blocks north of the Washington Monument, Baltimore Theatre Project presents festivals and performances in an ornate building built in 1883 for a completely different purpose.

It was a men's club, said Robert Mrozek, a New York City resident who began working at the Baltimore theatre in 1986 and who served as its producing director from 1990 to 2001.

It's a peculiar building," Robert said, mentioning its architectural oddities and the stage's acoustical band shell, which amplifies the slightest whisper and is one of only four remaining in North America.

Admitting his fascination with local history, the Baltimore native said he conducted research on the background of the building. He discovered that it was erected by the Improved Order of Heptasoths (IOH), which means seven wise men in neo-Greek, and added that in the late 19th century that area of the city was home to a large number of clubs and societies.

The Heptasoths assembly hall and lecture room now serves as the theatre's stage and audience area, but IOH logos and emblems are engraved into the building's interior walls and can be seen from the street on the building's stained glass windows and the brown capstone over the front entrance doorway.

The piano player tale, Robert said, was a recurring story throughout his time working in the building.

"I've never seen a ghost," he said, "but reports about the piano player occurred about two or three times a year. People would either hear music playing or see someone playing the piano. The comments came at different times from different people who could not have collaborated on their stories."

A typical situation would be someone saying to Robert, "I didn't know you played the piano," which he doesn't.

At other times, people would go into a room to rehearse and come out and report that someone, who was playing the piano, was using the space.

This latter situation sometimes caused people to become upset because they had scheduled the space and were annoyed that a piano player had cut into their time.

While admitting he had never seen the mysterious musician, Robert said the apparition was reported to be a male, who was tall and wearing a suit and tie. No one had ever identified the specific song being played, but the music was described as a rag, which would have been popular during the 1920s.

Incidentally, Robert said, during that era, the building was used as a dance hall, so the ghost might be from that period of time. One person who heard the phantom performer identified the music as a work by Schubert.

The unexplained activity would occur anywhere in the building," Robert said, since the piano was on wheels and was moved into the main theatre, backstage or out in the lobby. It also didn't matter if a piano was replaced, the ghostly musician played on any version of the instrument that was available.

The ghostly musican is said to perform on this and other pianos in the theatre.

"No one was ever terrified or frightened," Robert said. "They would just ask, 'Who was that guy?' One person said, 'I was finishing up my rehearsal and a guy came in to play the piano. And he was so good.' They may have thought it was peculiar, but no one was ever scared."

One wonders what Robert's response was to those who encountered the theatre's resident unpaid pianist.

"Eventually, I began to say, 'I guess that was the ghost piano player,' and the story began to circulate. When asked about it, I usually would smile and shrug. I enjoyed telling the story, and a lot of theatres have legends associated with them. It was a fun anecdote to get conversations started."

Since 2001, Anne Fulwiler has served as Theatre Project's director. While escorting me around the building, she admitted that she has never encountered the pianist and that here have been no unusual reports for the last few years.

The "IOH" initials can be seen in the windows and on the stonework of the building.

Despite the phantom pianist's recent reluctance to perform, his strange story seems to have taken on a mysterious life of its own.

For information on the Theatre Project, call (410) 752-8558 or visit the web site at www.theatreproject.org

Sources
Tom Chalkley, Charles Cohen and Brennen Jensen, "Baltimore's Ghost Stories to Tingle Your Spine," *Baltimore City Paper online*, October 25-31, 2000

Interview, Robert Mrozek, Theatre Project, April 2004

Interview, Anne Fulwiler, Theatre Project, April 29, 2004

Maryland's medical history is on display in Davidge Hall. Visitors also can learn about the school's early days, when some administrators and students were believed to be involved in grave robbing to support medical research.

112

Medical History and Grave Robbing

'It [grave robbing operation] was incredible. It would have made today's drug smugglers look like children.'—Larry Pitrof, Executive Director, Medical Alumni Association of the University of Maryland Inc.

There's a state historical marker at the busy intersection of Greene and Lombard streets. The metal sign stands beside the steps leading to Davidge Hall, the columned and domed 19th-century building named for Dr. John B. Davidge, first dean of Maryland's first medical school.

The marker states:

Noted for its classical appearance, it is the oldest building in the country used continuously for medical education. The medical school, established in 1807 by the Maryland General Assembly, was the fifth to be founded in the United States. Following mergers with Baltimore Medical College, 1913, and College of Physicians and Surgeons, 1915, the school became part of the state university system in 1920.

While interesting and informative, based on these details, Davidge Hall is not a site that the average seeker of legends, lore or ghost stories would place on a top-10 list. But looks—and historical markers, in particular—can be deceiving.

Certainly, there are only so many facts, and even fewer stories, that can fit on the marker's limited space. And historians

113

care more about dates, names and titles, as opposed to rumors, tales and legends. But those who take a moment to wander into Davidge Hall—now serving as home of The Medical Alumni Association of the University of Maryland—will find themselves transported into a much earlier era. And through historic artifacts, fascinating displays and noteworthy architecture (including a hidden stairway or two), the curious will learn about a period when medicine struggled for recognition and, at times, doctors and their students even feared for their lives.

Medicine, a not so glamorous profession

The focus of this chapter is the controversy that centered on dead bodies, which physicians needed for dissections. But, as Larry Pitrof explained, when the medical school began in the early 1800s doctors had not attained the level of respect and prestige that they hold today.

In the early 19th century, medicine was unregulated and those who were ill sought relief from a variety of sources, including barbershop surgeons, street corner apothecaries, men of the cloth who were believed to possess healing abilities and neighborhood practitioners of folk medicine.

Photo: Courtesy of Medical Alumni Association, U. of Md.

An early representation of Davidge Hall. Note the high walls, which were constructed to keep out mobs that might attack the building.

In addition, most people believed that when a person died, the body needed to be buried where it would rest undisturbed until the resurrection. And, if anyone dared open the corpse for medical examination, the soul would escape and be doomed to wander restlessly forever.

As a result of his role as executive director of the Medical Alumni Association of the University of Maryland for the last 10 years, Larry Pitrof displayed a commanding knowledge of Colonial-era medical practices. He spotlighted the college's outstanding alumni and their achievements, as well as the role of medicine in early American society. Then he shared startling stories about the school's extensive grave robbing enterprise.

In his second floor office in historic Davidge Hall, Larry talked candidly about a ghoulish method of securing bodies for research that most modern day administrators would tend to sweep under the rug. But, he added, staff and officials at the 19th century University of Maryland were not the only physicians and researchers involved in body snatching. The practice occurred at other medical schools throughout this country and in Europe as well.

There was a strong sense of skepticism about the value of trained physicians—and fanatical opposition to medical research using dead bodies— when Dr. Davidge began teaching out of a building beside his home. In fact, people sometimes demonstrated their outrage in violent ways.

According to Larry, the doctor had been teaching medicine in secret at his home for about a week when two youngsters, who had climbed onto the roof, looked down into the building through a skylight. They saw Davidge and his students

Photo: Courtesy of Medical Alumni Association, U. of Md.

Dr. John B. Davidge, first dean of Maryland's first medical school

studying a cadaver and the boys ran off and reported the story
to others.

"Within two hours," Larry said, "a mob gathered outside the
home and they tore down the building."

The medical school at Greene and Lombard streets was built
a few years later in what was a rural area at the time. This was
so the medical community's activities would be conducted a
distance from the center of town and, therefore, be less subject
to the scrutiny of angry city residents.

It wasn't until the 1880s, Larry said, that Maryland law per-
mitted agencies to turn over unclaimed bodies to the college for
medical research.

In search of . . . bodies

In the interim, teaching doctors and researchers had to resort
to other means to find cadavers to educate students in anatomy.

From approximately 1807 to the 1880s, grave robbing proved
to be an illegal, but necessary and workable, option. It was also
convenient. Within walking distance of the medical college, a
number of nearby cemeteries offered a steady supply of cadavers
to meet the ongoing educational demand.

"We were robbing graves at Westminster Burying Ground
and anywhere else we could get cadavers," Larry said.

In recent years, "Frank the Grave Robber" has been the
name used to present a composite image of all of the body
snatchers employed and used by the Maryland medical college,
which, at that time, Larry said, was paying about $20 for a body.

"It's believed students also participated in the practice," he
added, and there even were professional grave robbers who
were available for hire.

No doubt a variety of methods were used to discover a fresh
corpse and then extricate the body efficiently from its "eternal"
resting place. However, both Larry and Lu Ann Marshall, who
presents cemetery and catacombs tours at nearby Westminster
Burying Ground, offered a similar version of how "Frank" and
his body snatching colleagues would harvest their merchandise.

The grave robber would follow the horse drawn hearse and
funeral procession to the graveyard and observe the scene, paying close attention to the position of the body as it was lowered
into the ground. (This was critical to the speedy and efficient
removal of the corpse.)

That evening, the grave robber would arrive in the cemetery and, as Lu Ann pointed out, carefully note the position of any stones or special items of tribute that had placed atop the mound by family and friends. (These would be replaced in the proper order after the body was removed to cover up any evidence of the nighttime visit.)

Since he had noted the position of the corpse as it was placed in the ground at the graveside ceremony, the robber would dig up only the portion of the grave above the head of the coffin. When he reached the box, he would smash open the lid. Finally, he used a curved, butcher-style meat hook, which was placed under the cadaver's chin. With a sharp yank, the prize was lifted swiftly from the hole in the earth.

"Literally," Larry said, "in a couple of minutes the body would out of the ground and on its way. They were very proficient."

After replacing the dirt and returning the mementoes to their proper position, Frank would toss the body over a shoulder and race with it through back alleys and along dimly lit streets, arriving at the side doors of Davidge Hall.

According to The History Channel documentary *Secret Passages*, when renovations were conducted at Westminster Church, workmen—who had to dig foundations for the church in the old graveyard—reported that several of the graves in the Burying Ground were empty.

Lu Ann and Larry agreed that Westminster Burying Ground was convenient, being only two blocks from the medical school. But, they said, body snatchers also raided other city cemeteries.

To be useful for anatomical dissections, Larry explained, bodies had to be secured soon after the burial. Knowing this, cemeteries built walls to keep grave robbers out. Also, families hired guards that would stand beside new gravesites, remaining on watch until enough time had passed for decomposition to begin. This was done to protect loved ones from being carted off. (Embalming did not come into practice until the Civil War.)

Frank and his colleagues carried their cadaver contraband up two narrow winding stairways to the third floor of Davidge Hall. Today, in a cramped alcove hidden from the main hallway on the building's top floor, an old barrel stands beside the edge of the staircase. Dissections were conducted in this confined area

117

and the appropriate organs were removed for study, which would take place in the nearby amphitheater named Anatomical Hall.

Larry explained that the round wooden container is a replica of the all-purpose barrels that were used to store and also ship dead bodies.

Supplying a demand

The Maryland college's janitorial staff by day and grave robbing operators by night were very efficient. They were so good at their part time job that local corpses were sold and shipped to schools in need of cadavers as far away as New England.

A letter (the original of which no longer exists)—from Dr. Nathan R. Smith, professor of surgery at Maryland, to Dr. Parker Cleaveland of Bowdoin College in Maine—praises the proficiency of the Baltimore college's grave robbing staff.

The letter, dated September 25, 1830, states:

> *My Dear Sir:*
>
> *It will give me pleasure to render you any assistance in regard to subjects. I think you may rely upon having them. I shall immediately invoke Frank, our body snatcher (a better man never lifted a spade), and confer with him on the matter. We can get them without any difficulty at present, but I would not tell the world that any but ourselves should know that I have winked at their being sent out of state.*
>
> *I will cause about three to be put up in barrels of whiskey. I suppose they will require about half a barrel each of whiskey. This, at 35 cents a gallon, will be $16.50. The barrels, a dollar each; the subjects, the putting up, etc., making in all $50.*
>
> *Nathan R. Smith, M.D.*

During her catacombs tours at nearby Westminster Burying Ground, Lu Ann states that Frank surely visited the site often and he probably did his moonlighting work there on a steady basis.

Since police and family scrutiny of the medical school staff was highest immediately after a funeral, Larry said, sometimes Frank would have to hide the body for a short time. To preserve the specimen until it was safe to make delivery, the corpse would be stuffed into a barrel filled with whiskey.

Lu Ann added that after the body was removed from the alcohol filled keg, Frank would sell the whiskey to unknowing local saloonkeepers or to naïve medical students.

"That's where the term 'rot gut whisky' comes from," she said, smiling.

According to Larry, even though the grave robbing continued with some regularity for nearly 80 years, there were no prosecutions. In light of the public and law enforcement's awareness of the practice, that seems hard to believe.

"It was incredible," Larry said. "It would have made today's drug smugglers look like children."

This barrel on the third floor is a replica of those used to store and ship bodies that were needed for medical research.

Getting rid of the evidence was important. Disposal was done using cremation in an incinerator in the rear of the building. When the mechanism was dismantled in 1994, Larry said workers found bone fragments around the perimeter.

Reporting medicine's early history

Many would expect college officials to try to cover up the gruesome past associated with Davidge Hall, but instead present administrators speak candidly about the school's history. Several representatives' comments are featured in the History Channel documentary, entitled *Secret Passages*.

Addressing this issue, Larry said, "We're obligated to tell the true story of medicine here. It may not always be rosy and fuzzy. But it's a part of our lives and we shouldn't ignore it.

"Today, the medical profession is associated with prestige, acceptance and validation. When students enter into medical education, they are introduced to cadavers and know they are plentiful, and it's noble to dissect a body for medical science.

119

Many don't realize that 200 years ago there was a black market operation to secure what they take for granted today."

And while fascinating, the grave robbing aspect of medical history is only a small part of the Maryland medical college story. Larry spoke about the advances in medical practices and technology that today occur at a rapid rate. But, he said, visitors to Davidge Hall actually see an historic structure where medicine in this country began and, therefore, gain a better understanding of its development and future.

"We're excited about what we have here," Larry said, "and the fact that this building is still standing. You won't find another building that houses so much medical history anywhere else. We feel this is an added incentive of coming here. Samuel Mudd graduated here in 1856," Larry said, pointing to the numbered wooden chairs surrounding Chemical Hall, "He sat in one of these chairs, and later he treated John Wilkes Booth, one of the most famous assassins in American history. This shell of history here shares important links with the past."

While other medical colleges may have a single room devoted to its historical beginnings, Larry said the Maryland college in the center of Baltimore has maintained the complete building where its story began.

"Physicians who visit Davidge Hall," he said, "are thrilled that this structure exists and that it continues to function. They are absolutely delighted."

Ghost and legends

One question remained: Are there any ghost stories or sightings associated with Davidge Hall?

Surely with all the grave robbing and secrecy there must be some startling tales of hazy apparitions, creaking doors and unexplained footsteps or rolling barrels in the night.

Nodding, Larry acknowledged that he had heard the questions before. However, he explained that the desire of the school is to keep the emphasis on science, as opposed to myth.

Members of film production companies who have worked in the building and people who claim they can communicate with the dead have asked him the very same question. But he said he has experienced no sightings, nor has he heard of any ghost stories related to the historic building.

Finally, speaking as one who spends a significant amount of time working—often alone—in the historic structure, Larry added, "I do admit, however, that hearing noises in the building at night when I am here alone can be very unnerving."

For information on Davidge Hall, its tours and exhibits, or The Medical Alumni Association of the University of Maryland Inc., call (410) 706-7454 or send an e-mail message to mma@medalumni.umaryland.edu The building is open to the public from 8 a.m.-5 p.m. daily, Monday through Friday, and hosts about 5,000 visitors a year.

Interesting facts:

History

Davidge Hall is the oldest building in the United States that is continuously used for medical education. The building hosts lectures, symposia and also special events. When it was built, the surrounding wall was as high as 15 feet, since doctors at times feared for their lives.

Dr. John B. Davidge, the founder and first dean, was born in Annapolis and educated in Scotland.

The college was the first in the country to have a separate medical library for its students, as opposed to a section of the school library devoted to medicine.

Chartered in 1807, it is the fifth oldest medical school in the United States and the first medical school in the southern part of the U.S. Initially, the doctors taught students in their homes. Davidge Hall was built in 1812, and the building was placed on the National Register of Historic Places and was designated a National Historic Landmark in 1997.

Alumni

There were five students in the college's first graduating class in 1810. The Medical Alumni Association was established in 1875 and currently has 7,000 living alumni.

Chemical Hall, located on the first floor, has a kiosk where visitors can activate the History Channel documentary dealing with Davidge Hall's history, medicine during the 19th century and grave robbing practices.

121

Two noteworthy alumni of the college who sat in the chairs in the first level amphitheater include Dr. Samuel A. Mudd, who set the broken leg of John Wilkes Booth, and was a graduate of the class of 1856; and James Carroll, of the class of 1891, who identified the cause of yellow fever. A display related to his finding and letters of congratulation from Walter Reed are featured in a hall display on the third floor.

Architecture and Exhibits

The college's first honorary degree of doctor of laws was presented on October 9, 1824, to Revolutionary War hero Gen. Marquis de Lafayette. In Anatomical Hall, on the third floor, a gold metal disc (see photo on next page) in the center of the floor marks the occasion and the spot. However, more fascinating is what occurs when one stands on the disc and speaks. Because of the architectural precision employed during the building's construction, one's voice is amplified to a level equal to using an electronic loudspeaker. This was a major benefit for both lecturer and students. A visit to Davidge Hall is incomplete if one does not experience this marvelous acoustical/architectural feature.

Photo: Courtesy of Medical Alumni Association, U. of Md.

Anatomical Hall, is located on the third floor of Davidge Hall. Note the disk in the center of the floor. (An enlargement is on the next page.)

Patterned after the many anatomical theatres used in Europe, a series of skylights provided illumination in days before electricity.

One of the most asked questions: How long did it take to earn a medical degree? Two years, and the thesis was presented in Latin.

The Akiko Kobayashi Bowers Collection of Medical Artifacts is displayed it the building. It includes portraits, busts, books and medical instruments dating back to the earliest days of organized medicine in the country.

The building houses one of the most complete opthamological collections of spectacles, lorgnettes, monocles and glasses in the world.

In the third-floor alcove, not far from the large barrel that transported corpses, is a glass case containing Hermie. This is the name given to a cadaver that arrived at the school 1960 of a person born in 1895. When prospective medical students visit the building, Larry said he is sure to include an introduction to Hermie in the tour, so potential doctors can see what they eventually will be involved in. "That's when some of them decide to become lawyers," he said.

Sources:

Haunted Baltimore, The History Channel Documentary

Interview, Larry Pitrof, Executive Director of the Medical Alumni Association of the University of Maryland, June 2004

TEACHERS

Help your students learn and enjoy *history by using 'Baltimore GHOSTS' in your classroom.*

Our *Baltimore GHOSTS and HISTORY Teacher's Guide* includes graphic organizers, exercises, vocabulary, reproducibles, and activities that are ideal for immediate use in your classroom.

Baltimore
GHOSTS and HISTORY

Teacher's Guide
by Cassandra Cogan
8th Grade
Special Education Teacher

Baltimore
GHOSTS

Based on the book
Baltimore Ghosts
Feature, History Legend and Lore
by Ed Okonowicz

Created by Cassandra Cogan, an 8th grade special education teacher, this guide helps teachers focus on history by keeping students entertained and interested.

8 1/2" x 11"
$8.95

Nearly 40% of Americans believe in ghosts.

(Ed Okonowicz)

128 pages
5 1/2" x 8 1/2"
softcover
ISBN 1-890690-08-2
$9.95

Find out why, in this collection of true tales and eerie fiction, featuring

• Five college football players who fled their ghost infested apartment
• A troubled beach home in Lewes, Delaware, and a very strange house near the C & D Canal
• A haunted cottage near Hancock Bridge, site of a New Jersey Revolutionary War massacre
• A haunted supermarket, ghost dog, phantom military car, eerie barn and the Pig Woman legend
• The tale of Colonial-era Chief Justice Samuel Chew, who would not rest until he was buried—twice
• Pesky phantoms at a Georgia Plantation Cotton Field, in a story by Jaime Cherundolo
. . . and a lot more.

. . . and you thought sharks were the only danger at the beach!

In *Terrifying Tales of the Beaches and Bays* and the sequel, award-winning author and storyteller Ed Okonowicz shares eerie accounts of spirits roaming the shore.

Read about:

- A river pilot's memorable New Year's Eve cruise
- Desperate Confederates escaping from an island prison
- Serious seekers of pirate gold
- Fishermen stranded in the icy Chesapeake Bay
- Lighthouse keepers still tending a long-gone beacon
- A most unusual "catch of the day"
- Ocean City's "Trash Rat"
- and more . . . .

128 pages
5 1/2" x 8 1/2"
softcover
ISBN 1-890690-06-6

$9.95 each

A Delmarva beach-reading best seller in 2001

128 pages
5 1/2" x 8 1/2"
softcover
ISBN 1-890690-10-4

48 pages
5 1/2" x 8 1/2"
softcover
ISBN 1-890690-07-4
$6.95

Treasure Hunting
by Eddie Okonowicz

Dig up your own hidden treasures with this excellent "how to" book

This book is loaded with tips on using a metal detector to hunt for relics and treasure, plus photos of numerous historical finds.

True
Ghost Stories from Master Storyteller Ed Okonowicz

*S*pirits
Between the Bays
Series

Volume by volume we built this haunted house book series.
Enter at your own risk!

Wander through the rooms, hallways and dark corners of this eerie collection.

Creep deeper and deeper into terror, and learn about the area's history in our series of ghostly tales and folklore from states in the Mid-Atlantic region.

For detailed information on each volume, visit our web site

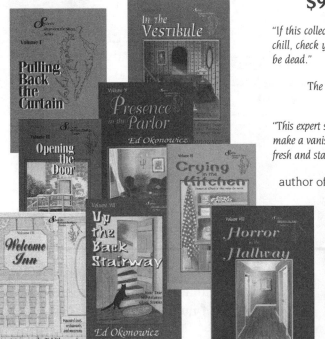

$9.95 each

"If this collection doesn't give you a chill, check your pulse, you might be dead."
—Leslie R. McNair
The Review, University of Delaware

"This expert storyteller can even make a vanishing hitchhiker story fresh and startling."
—Chris Woodyard
author of *Haunted Ohio* series

POSSESSED OBJECTS PLAGUE THEIR OWNERS

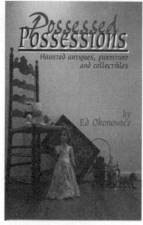

112 pages
5 1/2" x 8 1/2"
softcover
ISBN 0-9643244-5-8

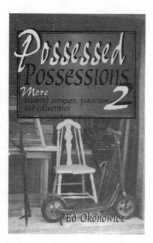

112 pages
5 1/2" x 8 1/2"
softcover
ISBN 0-890690-02-3

$9.95 each

Read about them in *Possessed Possessions* and *Possessed Possessions* **2** the books some antique dealers *definitely* do not want you to buy.

A BUMP. A THUD. MYSTERIOUS MOVEMENT. Unexplained happenings. Caused by What? Venture through this collection of short stories and discover the answer. Experience 20 eerie, true tales about items from across the country that, apparently, have taken on an independent spirit of their own—for they refuse to give up the ghost.

From Maine to Florida, from Pennsylvania to Wisconsin—these haunted heirlooms exist among us—everywhere.

"If you're looking for an unusual gift for a collector of antiques, or enjoy haunting tales, this one's for you."
—Collector Editions

"This book is certainly entertaining, and it's even a bit disturbing."
—Antique Week

". . . an intriguing read."
—Maine Antique Digest

WARNING

There could be more than just dust hovering around some of the items in your home.

Disappearing Delmarva

Portraits of the Peninsula People

Photography and stories by Ed Okonowicz

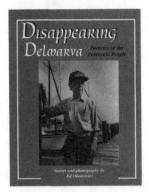

Disappearing Delmarva introduces you to more than 70 people on the peninsula whose professions are endangered. Their work, words and wisdom are captured in the 208 pages of this hardbound volume, which features more than 60 photographs.

Along the back roads and back creeks of Delaware, Maryland, and Virginia—in such hamlets as Felton and Blackbird in Delaware, Taylors Island and North East in Maryland, and Chincoteague and Sanford in Virginia—these colorful residents still work at the trades that have been passed down to them by grandparents and elders.

208 pages
8 1/2" x 11"
Hardcover
ISBN 1-890690-00-7

$38.00

Friends, Neighbors & Folks Down the Road

Photography and stories by
Ed Okonowicz & Jerry Rhodes

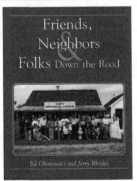

From small towns and villages in Lancaster County, Pa., Cecil County, Md., and New Castle, Kent and Sussex counties in Delaware, there are dozens of unique, surprising and entertaining characters waiting to be discovered in the stories and nearly 150 photographs in this book. They all prove that there are fascinating people worth knowing about, who are located right down the road and around the bend.

208 pages
8 1/2" x 11"
Hardcover
ISBN 1-890690-12-0

$30.00

"*. . . fun-to-read coffee-table book*"
—*Delaware Today Magazine*

"*Reading the first chapter is like finding a $20 bill in the pocket of your jeans on laundry day; unexpected, a pleasant surprise, an omen of good things to come.*"
—David Healey, *The Cecil Whig*